PRAISE FOR *CRACKING THE COACHING CODE*

"Thank you for putting together an awesome coaching resource. After being in this game for over 25 years at various levels, including the last 23 at the College level, this book lays out all the different personality types you will run into. Mental health and mental training are huge factors in our sport, and this lays out different strategies on how to deal with situations that cause mental anguish among athletes, coaches, administrators, and parents. This is definitely a book all coaches, new and old, should use to help gain an advantage and help our players and programs."

–**Brett Kelley, head baseball coach, Illinois Central College**

"Dr. Caposey and Dr. Wills have really challenged the way I approach coaching athletes and other coaches through their teachings in this book. For any coaches out there looking for an edge, *Cracking the Coaching Code* should be a must-have on your bookshelf."

–**Andrew Bartman, director, Coaching Development for USA Baseball**

"Dr. Caposey and Dr. Wills have put together a must read for coaches across all sports at all levels. Their deep dive into self-awareness for coaches and discovering the varied personalities of individual team members will help create successful coaches in all arenas. Successful coaching is discovering and managing the personalities of team members, and they have established the blueprint for that type of success."

–**Craig Anderson, executive director, Illinois High School Association**

"As recruiting coordinator for a junior-college baseball team, I wanted a test to make sure potential recruits had the traits our staff felt made us most successful. It turns out we should have been meeting the kids where they were, and *Cracking the Coaching Code* would have allowed us to do just that! A tremendous learning and teaching tool!"

–**Ben Diggle, owner, Diggle's Diamonds Recruiting Service, associate scout, Cincinnati Reds**

"Coaches want their players to continually improve. This is a book for coaches who want to do the same. PJ and Bryan provide the framework and tools to help you better understand your athletes, better understand yourself, and become a better coach".

–Joe Kilbride, business consultant and high school basketball coach with five Final Fours and two state championships in 9 years of IHSA Class 4A state tournaments.

"As a College Baseball Coach for nearly 4 decades and USA 18U National Coach, I'm excited about what *Cracking the Coaching Code* can do for all coaches and athletes. This well thought out blueprint, along with the stories, insights, and experiences, are great teaching tools for becoming more successful coaches, athletes, and people! A thoughtful read to improve your everyday life!"

–Jack Leggett, 38-year college baseball coach, 18 U National Team Manager (20180–2019), ABCA Hall of Famer 2014

CRACKING THE COACHING CODE
Using Personality Archetypes to Maximize Performance

By PJ Caposey and Bryan Wills

ROWMAN & LITTLEFIELD
Lanham • Boulder • New York • London

Published by Rowman & Littlefield
An imprint of The Rowman & Littlefield Publishing Group, Inc.
4501 Forbes Boulevard, Suite 200, Lanham, Maryland 20706
www.rowman.com
86-90 Paul Street, London EC2A 4NE
Copyright © 2023 by PJ Caposey and Bryan Wills
All rights reserved. No part of this book may be reproduced in any form or by any electronic or mechanical means, including information storage and retrieval systems, without written permission from the publisher, except by a reviewer who may quote passages in a review.

British Library Cataloguing in Publication Information Available

Library of Congress Cataloging-in-Publication Data
Names: Caposey, PJ, author. | Wills, Bryan, 1976- author.
  Title: Cracking the coaching code : using personality archetypes to maximize performance / by PJ Caposey and Bryan Wills.
  Description: Lanham, Maryland : Rowman & Littlefield, 2023. | Includes bibliographical references. | Summary: "This book gives coaches real world tools, applications, and lessons to help them become their best self and tap the full potential of their athletes; turning them into successful and productive men and women"-- Provided by publisher.
  Identifiers: LCCN 2023009852 (print) | LCCN 2023009853 (ebook) | ISBN 9781475871777 (cloth) | ISBN 9781475871784 (paperback) | ISBN 9781475871791 (epub)
  Subjects: LCSH: Coaching (Athletics)--Psychological aspects. | Performance--Psychological aspects.
  Classification: LCC GV711 .C323 2023 (print) | LCC GV711 (ebook) | DDC 796.07/7--dc23/eng/20230407
LC record available at https://lccn.loc.gov/2023009852
LC ebook record available at https://lccn.loc.gov/2023009853

Contents

Acknowledgments vii
Preface ix

Introduction 1
CHAPTER 1: Enneagram 101 5
CHAPTER 2: Tips on How to Use This Book 17
CHAPTER 3: Type 1 Deep Dive 25
CHAPTER 4: Type 2 Deep Dive 37
CHAPTER 5: Type 3 Deep Dive 53
CHAPTER 6: Type 4 Deep Dive 69
CHAPTER 7: Type 5 Deep Dive 85
CHAPTER 8: Type 6 Deep Dive 101
CHAPTER 9: Type 7 Deep Dive 115
CHAPTER 10: Type 8 Deep Dive. 131
CHAPTER 11: Type 9 Deep Dive. 143
CHAPTER 12: Self-Awareness 159
CHAPTER 13: Team and Staff Awareness 171
CHAPTER 14: Situational Awareness. 185
CHAPTER 15: Call to Action. 191

The Next Step 195
About the Authors. 197

Acknowledgments

I would like to thank my wife, Jacquie, and our four children: Jameson, Jackson, Caroline, and Anthony. First and foremost, thank you for loving me unconditionally and supporting my efforts to continue to influence the lives of others. Second, thank you all for sacrificing time with me in order to allow me to pursue my dreams.

My hope is that this book resonates with the five of you. Our bonds have been so forged through athletics that this small attempt to make the world of youth, high school, and college athletics a little bit better was absolutely done with you in mind. I love you.

—PJ

First and foremost, I would like to thank my wife, Stacy, and our two children: Brady and Alexa. It would be impossible for me to chase after my goals and dreams without all of your unconditional love, support, and encouragement. You are the fire that fuels my passion to make a difference in the lives of others.

Second, I'd like to thank my parents, Mark and Linda, my first coaches and biggest fans. So much of who I am today was built through all the sports you let me play growing up. Thank you for all the rides, all the sacrifices, all the celebrations when I won, and, more importantly, for all the pep talks when I lost.

Lastly, I'd like to thank all the incredible coaches I have had from pee-wee wrestling through college football. You never know the impact you have on the kids you coach. The lessons I learned from youth sports have carried me through my life. My hope is that this book will inspire

Acknowledgments

the next generation of coaches to mold kids into successful men and women.

—Bryan

Preface

I love sports. I love everything about them. From the competition to the camaraderie to the growth I experienced as a human being through athletics—I simply love all of it. Thus, as soon as my first son was born, I daydreamed about the ability to coach his team.

Seven years later, the time had come for me to start to pay forward all that my coaches had given to me. My son decided to play basketball, and while I was a wrestler in high school, I played basketball in junior high and had a high level of respect for the sport. Also, I thought it would probably be impossible to be underqualified to coach U8 basketball.

Now, my gut told me that I was taking this responsibility a bit too seriously. I was hyper-organized. My background as an entrepreneur, business owner, and executive coach led me to have fully detailed practice plans before the first practice. Once my wife got wind of this, she confirmed what my gut had told me earlier, but I was undeterred. In fact, I was pretty confident that I was going to be the best darn U8 basketball coach our area had ever seen.

I walked into practice on the first day with the revised version of the original practice plan. Every minute was accounted for. I mean, seriously, Nick Saban would have been proud of this practice plan. Kids and parents started to shuffle in a few minutes before practice began, and I made the obligatory small talk, but what I wanted to do was to watch my players. The minutes seemed to last for hours until, finally, it was time. I blew my whistle and called the kids to center court. *I was coaching!*

We did a quick introduction, then I slowly introduced the first skill we would be practicing. As I introduced this basic drill to second and third graders, I was embarrassingly nervous. I even kept looking down at the practice plan, though I had it just about memorized.

First, I told them about the drill. Then, I showed them the drill. Then, I had my son demonstrate the drill. And then, it was time to let the rest of the team have a shot at this. Things had gone exactly to plan, and I was still on pace with my practice plan!

It took about ten seconds to realize that I was in way over my head. The kids were running around all over the place. Some were kicking basketballs like soccer balls to each other; others were running with the balls like footballs. And it still looked like the only dribbling they had ever done was with ice cream down the front of their shirts.

I was immediately and abruptly humbled. I stayed the course for a while, but everything I had planned in my head (and on paper) was simply not working. Trying to get them to get in a line or to partner up was a Herculean effort. I could feel the frustration and anger building inside me, but I somehow made it through the longest hour of my life.

I went home that night with an intense fear in the form of the question, "What am I going to do with nine more weeks of this?" When I shared my frustration and concern with my wife, she quipped, "I thought you had the perfect practice plan designed!" This brought forth some much-needed laughter, but my mind was consumed. I was not thinking about my business or my clients, I was thinking about how I could better get through to this group of seven- and eight-year-old kids.

I spent the night thinking about all the coaches I had had from little league through college. I have had many men and women leave an indelible impact on my life. Some good, and some bad. But one coach stood above the others during my night's long meditation on how to deal with my current situation—my high school track coach.

My high school track coach always seemed to be playing chess when everyone else around him was playing checkers. He had a way of making everyone feel known and valued, while also pushing them to their limits. He forever changed my life when he placed absolute trust in me in one of the most intense athletic moments of my life.

My relay team had made it to the state finals in the 4 x 400-meter relay. Not only had we made it into the finals, but going into the championship race, we had one of the fastest times in the state. We had a legitimate shot at the title. I will never forget the feeling I had in my stomach before hearing the opening gun for that race.

I ran the second leg of the relay, which meant that I had to run the first one hundred meters in our lane after I got the baton, and then cut to the inside lane of the track. This leg required a unique skill set—or at least that is what my coach made me believe. Coach always emphasized to me that I was chosen to run this leg because, while I wasn't the fastest sprinter on the team, I was stubborn, competitive, and played football, so I was used to a little contact, which always happens when everyone is jockeying for position on the back stretch. I always appreciated his honesty with me as an athlete and the trust he put in me to do this unique job.

On the third curve, another runner, who happened to be from the town next to ours and our fiercest rival, tried to pass me. As had been beaten into my head by my coach, you never let someone pass you when you run this race. It took everything I had, but I held him just off my shoulder, so he would wear himself out on the curve.

Unfortunately, he became impatient and tried to cut in front of me, kicking my foot toward the center rail of the track. I stepped on the rail and fell. In one step, four years of hard work went down the drain. In one step, dreams were smashed. After the fall, my instincts kicked in, and, in a daze, I got back up and tried frantically to catch up to the pack. We were already too far behind though and finished in last place.

The four of us stood on the infield in stunned disbelief. All our hard work that season had been in vain because of a foul. In the moment, there was disappointment and confusion; we were unsure if the officials would see the contact as a foul and, if they did, what the recourse would be. We just stood together in the moment. Another thing I love about athletics is that, in that moment, we were fully and absolutely together in a way many people cannot even begin to fathom.

After what felt like an hour later, but was much closer to a minute later, our coach ran over and said we had a choice. The other team had been disqualified, so we could either take our eighth-place medal, or run the race by ourselves, and whatever time we got would dictate our place.

However, if we dropped the baton or somehow were disqualified, we would not get a state medal.

"So, what do you want to do?"

This was the moment and the question I alluded to earlier. The coach did not tell us what to do. He was asking us. And in actuality, he was not asking us—he was asking me.

At the start of every track season, Coach would set up practices to identify who the leaders of the group were. We would go on long runs through town, and he would have an assistant at certain checkpoints (that we couldn't see and that I did not even realize was there until after I had graduated) to make sure we did the whole loop. He would set up workouts with us separated into teams competing against each other. All of this was to see who would step up and take charge, and who needed to be pushed. Chess, not checkers—remember?

After four years of being put through all his "tests," he knew, and my teammates knew, whom to look to when the chips were down. This question was mine to answer. Everyone knew what I was going to say. There was no way my high school track career was going to end like this.

"We are running again!"

If this were a Disney movie, we would have set the school record and won a state championship. However, our truth was that, despite the most intense and awkward of circumstances, we finished as state medalists after running a race only against the clock and for a second time in a matter of minutes. While the circumstances were less than ideal, hearing thousands of people cheering only for you is an adrenaline rush you never forget.

We finished with the fourth-fastest time in the state and with a story I can tell for the rest of my life. After this walk down memory lane was complete, I started thinking less about the events of the track meet and more about my coach. I kept thinking about how he always seemed a step or two ahead of everyone else and every other coach I had. I needed to figure out what made him different, so that maybe, just maybe, I could get these seven- and eight-year-olds to stand in a straight line at the next practice.

I came to the realization that Coach did four things exceptionally well. One, he absolutely knew his athletes. Two, he had a great understanding of how his athletes interacted with each other and the dynamics of the multiple groupings that existed on our team. Three, he made sure his team understood situations, and that the same engagements on day one of practice would not suffice at the state championships. Four, he had a deep understanding of himself. He was fully in control of his emotions and was never a prisoner of the moment. He was more than just a coach—he was a leader.

Armed with my story and corresponding realizations, and with the understanding that I was dealing with seven- and eight-year-olds and not adults—after a firm reminder from my wife—I completely changed my approach.

I sought to get to know my athletes and my team. I adjusted to the situation and became hyper-aware of what I was trying to do *for me* compared to what I was trying to do *for them*. As a result, over the next couple of practices, we played a lot of games, had many laughs, and, eventually, they stood in a straight line—Watch out, Coach K!

During this time, I observed how the kids interacted with each other. I identified who the leaders of the group were; and when I wanted to teach a drill, I would have them at the front of the line showing everyone not only what to do but also that it can be done. Thankfully, the season went great and the kids really improved.

However, that would not have been possible if I had not taken the time to see my own shortcomings and to realize that, regardless of how hard I pushed, my "way" wasn't going to get the job done. I had to change not only what I was doing and how I saw the kids but also my perception of what the intended outcome of being a coach really was. It was not just about winning games or teaching a sport, it was about leading humans—in this case, little humans—forward.

Why Are We Writing This?

Many people, including both of us, identify their past coaches among the most influential people in their lives. Unfortunately, this is not always a positive experience.

Preface

With this awareness comes responsibility.

According to *The New York Times*, more than 45 million children in the United States are engaged in a sport at a young age, but 70 percent will quit playing by the age of thirteen. This happens for a variety of reasons, but there is no shortage of anecdotal evidence that coaching plays a large part in many of the decisions to quit participating.

Leaving athletics deprives young people of several opportunities for growth, but more troubling is the pressure many are feeling from participating in sports. "The professional consensus is that the incidence of anxiety and depression among scholastic athletes has increased over the past 10 to 15 years," says Marshall Mintz, a New Jersey-based sports psychologist who has worked with teenagers for thirty years. As one 2015 study by the National Athletic Trainers' Association found, "Many student-athletes report higher levels of negative emotional states than non-student-athlete adolescents." These findings are corroborated by a study done by the *British Journal of Sports Medicine* that shows that around 25 percent of all collegiate athletes show signs of depression. Other studies show different percentages, but, almost universally, the number significantly exceeds that of their nonathlete peers.

In our experience serving the education system—PJ, as a superintendent of schools, and Bryan, as a board of education president—we have seventy combined years, in one capacity or another, in the public education system. Upon our analysis, it has become readily apparent that one area of training and professional development that is clearly lacking within our school systems is the leadership development of our athletic coaches and activities advisors.

Said simply, we have an acute understanding that many athletes will have life-changing experiences with, and as a result of, their coaches, yet we invest far too little in that process. That must shift. This book is our attempt to start that conversation.

As co-authors, we are friends. We have found that, although we have a great deal in common in our personal and professional lives, our conversations often drift back to lessons learned in the athletic arena. We've discovered that we were both shaped, in many ways, by the coaches we have had, the moments we have experienced with teammates, and in the heat of competition.

Since both of us are directly linked to the education field, we have many conversations inside and outside of our trusted circles on the impact of schools and often discuss what we could do to help create a better system for our kids. Over time, we have both noticed how many people, when asked about the most influential person in their school-related lives, immediately respond with one of their coaches, not one of their teachers.

However, and as difficult as it is to hear, this isn't always a positive memory for people. Unfortunately, "most influential" does not always mean "most beneficial." It was this that led us down a road of research, discovery, and reflection of how insanely difficult it is to fulfill the job of being a coach. Then, as leaders in the educational realm, we came to the troubling realization that the most influential person in many of our students' lives, their coach(es), has received no formal training on leadership, relationships, and understanding personality archetypes.

We wanted to help be part of the solution, so we authored this book. We weave in personal stories and anecdotes, and combine the lessons we have learned in our own leadership and through our coaching of others to create a tool that we hope makes the difficult job of coaching easier. We hope to have cracked the code to enable coaches to have an even greater impact on the lives of their athletes.

Through our research, preparation, and conversations in the construction of the book, the actual difficulty of the job is what rang through most clearly to us. We felt we needed to start the book by honoring this, and there is no better way to do that in our opinions than through the Bill Parcells quote below:

> "It is a difficult job, and there is no clear way to succeed. One cannot copy another who is a winner for there seems to be some subtle, secret chemistry of personality that enables a person to lead successfully and no one really knows what it is. Those who have succeeded and those who have failed represent all kinds—young and old. Inexperienced and experienced, hard

and soft, tough and gentle, good natured and foul tempered, proud and profane, articulate and inarticulate, even dedicated and casual. Some are smarter than others, but intelligence is not enough. All want to win, some want to win more than others, and just winning is often not enough. Losers almost always get fired, but winners get fired too.

He/she is out in the open being judged publicly almost every day or night for six, seven, or eight months a year by those who may or may not be qualified to judge them. And every victory and every defeat is recorded constantly in print or on the air and periodically totaled up.

A coach has no place to hide. He/she cannot just let the job go for a while or do a bad job and assume no one will notice, as most of us can.

A coach cannot satisfy everyone; seldom can the coach even satisfy very many. Rarely can the coach satisfy themselves.

If a coach wins once, they must win the next time too

Coaches plot victories, suffer defeats, and endure criticism from within and without. They neglect their families, travel endlessly and live alone in a spotlight surrounded by others. Theirs may be the worst profession—unreasonably demanding, and insecure and full of unrelenting pressures. Why do they put up with it? Why do they do it?

Having seen them hired and hailed as geniuses at gaudy parting like press conferences and having seen them fired with phrases such as 'fool' or 'incompetent.' I have wondered about them. Having seen them exultant in victory and depressed by defeat. I have sympathized with them. Having seen some broken by the job and others die from it, one is moved to admire them and hope that someday the world will learn to understand them."

—Bill Parcells (credit to Bill Libby)

Introduction

THE PATH FORWARD

We believe that two things set great coaches apart from their peers—one, incredible self-awareness, and two, an intimate awareness of their athletes as individuals *and* as a collective whole. This combination of understanding themselves and their team begets next-level situational awareness, which breeds ultimate success.

- Self—Great coaches know themselves. It is impossible to lead others if we are struggling to lead ourselves. As Stephen Covey has said, "Internal victory must take place before external victory."
- Athlete and Team—Great coaches sincerely know their athletes. They know them as individuals and as competitors. They understand what motivates them, what they fear, and how to pull the very best out of them. Moreover, great coaches know how their puzzle pieces fit together. A team is a collection of individuals, each with their own idiosyncrasies. Successful coaches understand how these individuals fit together and, most importantly, put them in positions to use each individual's strengths for the overall betterment of the entire group.
- Situational—The synthesis of self and team awareness in the coaching realm is situational awareness. Great coaches know that they will not be in control of all the events that impact their team. They are simply in charge of their response to those events. As a result, winning coaches adapt to the situation and put their

athletes in positions to learn and win. This is only possible when coaches deeply understand themselves and the athletes they have the privilege to coach.

We will continually reinforce the importance of awareness throughout this book and encourage readers to adopt the R^3 method to analyze and improve their performance. The three-step process represented with R^3 is "Review – Reset – Resolve." While a simple, three-step process may seem easy, it will certainly take diligent effort to deploy this strategy. Throughout the book, we will explore this concept, and believe it to be an effective and easy-to-understand strategy that coaches can use to assess and improve their awareness in real-time.

It is easy to read about great coaches and to backward-engineer what makes them amazing. It is much harder to attempt to create a system or protocol that will help any coach, whether it is a coach of a U8 basketball team or a team competing for a state championship, become a great coach.

Over the past fifteen years, we have been using a tool that facilitates incredible success when coaching other executives, administrators, and leaders. What we have found is that the same process used to maximize the leadership potential in other professional settings has the same ability to create outstanding coaches. This process hinges on using the Enneagram system to help identify personality styles and behavioral tendencies. This tool has allowed us to dramatically increase individual self-awareness and to help leaders better understand and adapt to the personality and behavioral patterns of those they lead. This process gives you the opportunity to review the situation you are in, reset your own emotions, and resolve the situation with the behavior that you feel will best match your intended outcome.

Why Is That the Best Solution?

Most of us have been in situations where we can't get a group of athletes we are coaching to gel together as a team and simply cannot figure out how to get the very best out of the athletes we have the privilege of leading. Enneagram is our Rosetta Stone to figuring out how to speak the language of each person we lead.

Enneagram serves as a system that helps you see how all the pieces fit together. More importantly, it helps you to understand how and why you might be getting in your own way of creating your path forward. We believe that better understanding your own default reactions to stress, your basic desires, and your basic fears will make you a better leader. Armed with this knowledge of self and expanding these insights to those you lead will catapult you to unprecedented levels of success.

How Are We Going to Do This?

The book will be broken down into three distinct sections. The first section (chapters 1–2) will be a short general overview of the Enneagram system. The Enneagram identifies the predominant personality profile of an individual and labels them as one of nine types. The second section of the book (chapters 3–11) will outline each of the nine types in detail. Each section will include sports-relevant examples and clear takeaways on how to best coach and interact with each personality type.

The final section of the book (chapters 12–14) will break down each of the awarenesses described throughout the introduction and give concrete steps for each coach to take to increase their aptitude in each area or provide concrete steps for a principal or athletic director to take to guide their coaches through the development process.

Lastly, in our call to action, we hope to inspire you to start positive forward momentum. Implementing significant change happens one day at a time. We also pay homage to the other aspects of the job that extend beyond simply working with your athletes. Our belief is that, if the reader deeply internalizes the meaning behind the lessons and strategies taught throughout this book, they can also be used situationally with parents, administration, and media.

Chapter 1

Enneagram 101

Often in life, we create our own storms, and then we get mad when it starts to rain. The problem is that we are typically unaware that the storm is coming, that we started it, and that only we can stop it.

Enneagram is a tool that can be used to increase self-awareness and ownership of behavior. As with all other work, internal victory is needed before external victory can take place. Since we are writing this for coaches, many people consuming this will immediately think of their athletes. While that is a key element to what we hope to accomplish, remember that internal victory is necessary first.

I learned this the hard way. I immediately fell in love with Enneagram when I was first introduced. I could not wait to "type" my people and my teams and get to work moving us toward peak performance. The issue was that I had not done the work to truly understand myself and the impact I was having on others first.

About four months into my Enneagram journey, I was far from an expert. Rationally looking back, this makes complete sense, but my behavior at that time did not match. I was overbearing and insensitive in my approach and delivery of the tool. I just had no idea.

One night I was doing some reading about my Enneagram type, and I came across a line that said my type tends to come across as condescending in meetings. My immediate instinct was to dismiss this piece of information for two reasons. First, I did not like the way it made me feel; and second, I had never heard this from any of my direct reports, athletes, or coworkers, so it must not be true.

However, the line stuck with me, ringing in my head and forcing me to ask myself the question, "Do I come across as condescending in meetings?" Finally, one day I was meeting with the team to whom I felt closest, and I knew this was my opportunity to find out. I knew that if anyone would be straight and honest with me, it was this group. So, at the end of a meeting, I simply asked the question.

Instantaneously, everyone turned into bobbleheads, nodding furiously and agreeing with the sentiment without saying a word. Then finally, someone spoke up and said that this trait of mine was never more pronounced than when I was introducing Enneagram. For weeks, I had wondered about their subtle resistance to this amazing tool. At that moment, I learned that they were not resisting Enneagram as I had suspected; they were resisting me.

I created my own storm and was upset when it started to rain. Enneagram helped me at that moment become more aware of the storm but, more importantly, has helped me avoid similar storms in the future as I continue my journey of self-development.

"He who knows others is learned. He who knows himself is wise."—Lao Tzu

What Is Enneagram?

The Enneagram is a system that categorizes personalities into nine different types. Each type has a distinct way of seeing the world and an underlying motivation that influences how that type thinks, feels, and behaves. The purpose of the Enneagram is not to change your personality type into one that you think is better; that is impossible. Rather, it is to develop a deep self-awareness of who you are and to identify the parts of your personality that limit you from being your truest and best self.

When I was first learning about Enneagram, one phrase really helped me make sense of it—"Your Enneagram type is who you are when you are on autopilot." As humans, we have the unique ability to experience an event, process it, choose our behavior before we react, and then move forward. Too often in life, we simply react based on our default personality without giving it much thought. Enneagram helps us eliminate this behavior to grow beyond the self-defeating dimensions of our personality and limit the storms we create in our lives, so we can be successful, both personally and professionally.

In other words, our personality does not have to dictate our behaviors. "That's just the way I am" is a missed opportunity for growth. Personality is not your destiny—it's your tendency.

The reason we have chosen the Enneagram over other types of personality profiles, like Myers Briggs, DISC, and Caliper, to name a few, is that the Enneagram takes into account the fluid nature of the personality, which is constantly adapting as circumstances change. Enneagram is dynamic, fluid, and functional. Personally, Enneagram has had an incredible impact on our personal and professional success, and on the teams we lead.

Before we begin with a brief technical introduction to Enneagram, it is important to note that while this book intends to teach you core concepts of Enneagram, the intent is to give you the tools necessary to be successful in using this tool to make you a better leader and coach. Therefore, while it is possible (and there are thousands of books already written about it) to write a book about Enneagram, that is not the primary function of this work. So, as we briefly introduce anything to do with the Enneagram, please know that there are more significant and thorough explanations available.

The Enneagram comes from the Greek words for nine (*ennea*) and for figure (*gram*). It is a nine-pointed geometric figure that illustrates the different but interconnected personality types. While we have all nine types within our personality, only one is predominant and dictates most of our behaviors. However, as you can see from the diagram below, each number on the circumference is connected to two others by arrows across the circle representing their dynamic interactions with one another.

The Enneagram tool has been around for thousands of years, but by most accounts was brought to the United States in the 1970s. In the mid-1970s, Don Riso and Russ Hudson began the study of Enneagram and helped move this tool into a far less niche corner of the world. What was almost unknown in this country fifty years ago is now a study with

CHAPTER 1

THE ENNEAGRAM

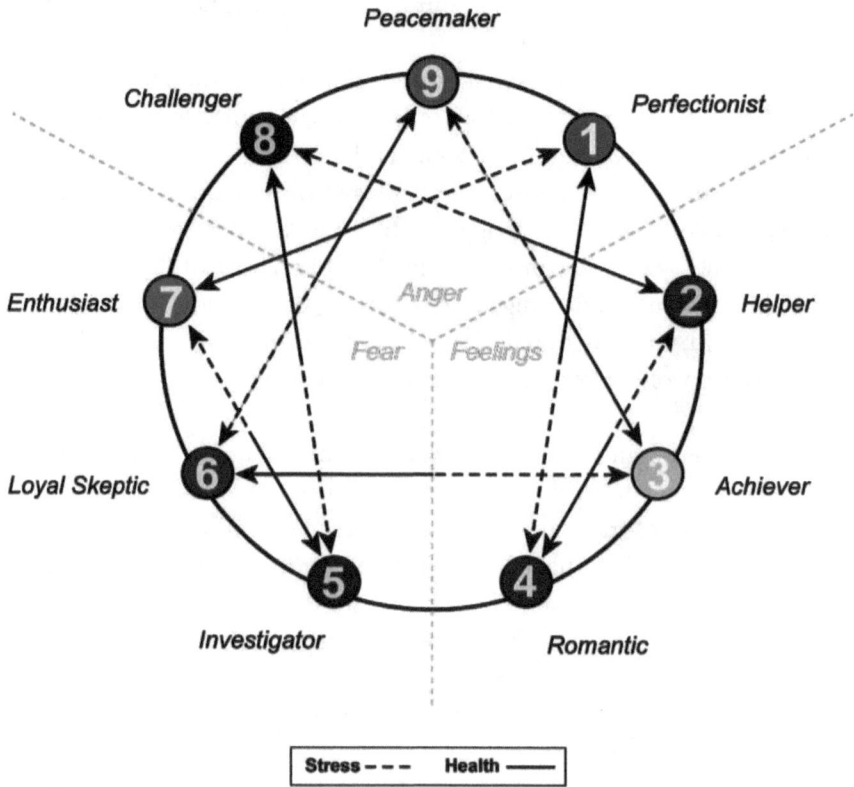

thousands of books written on it, used in corporate strategy for some Fortune 500 companies, and practiced in tens of thousands of schools and businesses across America. Recently, it has become more pronounced in the athletic world, as some schools have publicly announced using Enneagram as part of their recruiting of athletes.

Bottom line, Enneagram is growing in popularity and becoming more pervasive in popular culture and the educational, athletic, and corporate worlds.

By this point, if you are not familiar with Enneagram, you are probably wondering what these nine personality types entail. Below, I very briefly introduce each type. However, each type will have its own chapter with its team-related impact later in the book.

- **Type 1: The Perfectionist.** Ethical and dedicated. They appreciate standards, principles, and structure. They are motivated to live the right way, improve the world, and avoid fault and blame.
- **Type 2: The Helper.** Kind, generous, and self-sacrificing. They value relationships and helping others. They are motivated by the need to be loved and avoid acknowledging their own needs.
- **Type 3: The Achiever.** Success-oriented, image-conscious, and highly productive. They value achievement and strive to be the best. They are motivated by the need to be, or, at least, appear to be, successful and avoid failure.
- **Type 4: The Romantic.** Creative, sensitive, and moody. They value individualism and self-expression. They are motivated by the need to express their uniqueness, be authentic, and avoid being ordinary.
- **Type 5: The Investigator.** Analytical, independent, and private. They value being self-sufficient and making sense of the world around them. They are motivated by the need to gain knowledge, conserve energy, and avoid relying on others.
- **Type 6: The Questioner.** Loyal, team-oriented, and practical. They value security and belonging. They are motivated by the need to be safe and prepared.
- **Type 7: The Enthusiast.** Adventurous, fun, and spontaneous. They value freedom, being inspired, and taking opportunities as they present themselves. They are motivated by the need to experience life to its fullest and avoid pain.
- **Type 8: The Challenger.** Commanding, intense, and confrontational. They value having a sense of control, being direct, and having an impact. They are motivated by the need to be strong and avoid feeling weak or vulnerable.
- **Type 9: The Peacemaker.** Accommodating, accepting, and laid-back. They value stability, harmony, and getting along with

others. They are motivated by the need to keep the peace and avoid conflict.

IDENTIFYING YOUR TYPE

What most likely just occurred for you is that you wanted to self-identify exactly which type you are by reading a thirty-five-word description. Please do not attempt to self-identify yet. As you read the following chapters, you'll be continually tempted to type yourself off the behaviors of a certain number. However, it's not the behaviors that dictate your number!

Instead, it is the *motivation that drives the behaviors* or traits of each number that dictates which Enneagram type you are. For example, as coaches, we may see the exact same behavior or goal established by multiple athletes of different personalities. For ease of cross-sport comparison, let's say we have several athletes that would like to be team captain.

The goal and the behaviors exhibited may be remarkably similar; the difference is in the reason *why* they want that role/title. A Type 1 may want to be team captain so they can "fix" the team by instituting team rules, whereas a Type 3 may want to be captain for the image of being captain or being able to go home and share this information proudly with their parents. Different still is that a Type 8 may want to be team captain for the control and authority that the position and title afford them. This list could go on for each Enneagram type, but the point is simple—it's not what you do, but rather why you do it, that reveals your true personality.

While you are reading this and your interest is peaking in Enneagram, you will likely start to Google all things associated with this new learning. In doing so, you will find that there are many free assessments out there that will help you identify your Enneagram type. Additionally, there are more thorough and statistically valid assessments out there, as well.

These tests have significant value and can shorten the period of time necessary for you to identify your Enneagram type, which may lead to a quicker path to self-awareness. What we both know as coaches, however, is that for most people taking an assessment to zero in on their personality type is not necessary, and in some cases can even breed further confusion, as is explained in the next section.

EMBRACING YOUR TYPE

My first experience with Enneagram was when my boss came to me nearly fifteen years ago and told me to take an online assessment. When I was finished, my two highest-scoring areas were that of Type 3 and Type 8. After reading the descriptions of each, I quickly decided that being a Type 3 sounded much better to me, and I decided that is what I was going to be.

When my boss called me in to debrief about the assessment and I announced I was a Type 3, he laughed out loud. He was much more well-versed in Enneagram than I was, and he said I was as true-blue of a Type 8 as he had ever seen. I dug in and resisted and asserted that I thought I was right—I was a Type 3. Ironically, this is prototypical Type 8 behavior.

It took my wife taking the assessment on my behalf, and significant work in self-awareness, before I was able to realize that I was a Type 8. As my learning has continued, my initial resistance has turned into a total embrace of who I am.

As you are reading and trying to figure out who you are, it is important to understand that each type sucks. And each type is amazing. There is no correlation between being a successful coach or athlete and being a particular type. Some numbers do have some qualities that might make it a little easier to find success; but remember, the only person present for all the mistakes, problems, and misadventures in your life is you. In fact, the source of most of the problems in your life is you.

TRIADS

The nine different personalities on the Enneagram are divided into three triads based on how each type takes in, processes, and responds to life. The three triads are the Gut or Anger Triad, the Heart or Feeling Triad, and the Head or Fear Triad. However, the three numbers in each triad are driven in different ways by the dominant emotion of that triad.

The Anger or Gut Triad (Types 8, 9, 1)
These Enneagram types are driven by anger. Saying someone is driven by anger may be initially off-putting if you are first learning about Enneagram; so, if you do not like the term "driven," instead consider anger to be the dominant emotion that people in this triad feel. Type 8s externalize it, Type 9s forget it, and Type 1s internalize it. They take in and respond to life instinctually and from their gut.

The Feeling or Heart Triad (Types 2, 3, 4)
These types are driven by feelings, with their dominant emotion being shame. Type 2s focus on the feelings of others, while Type 3s have a hard time recognizing their own or others' feelings, and Type 4s focus internally on their own feelings. This triad takes in and relates to life from their heart.

The Fear or Head Triad (Types 5, 6, 7)
These three types are driven by thinking, and their dominant emotion is fear. Type 5s externalize the fear, Type 6s internalize it, and Type 7s force themselves to forget it by distracting themselves. Members of this triad tend to think and carefully plan their way through life in order to minimize their own anxiety.

WINGS AND STRESS/SECURITY NUMBERS
As stated earlier, the reason we prefer the Enneagram over other personality systems is that it offers endless "flavors" of personalities. It also takes into account the fluid nature of our personalities as we adapt to our constantly changing circumstances and environments. While your number and core motivation never change, your behavior will, undoubtedly, change at times. Enneagram gives us a deeper understanding of how and when this occurs.

Your behaviors will change based on your own emotional health and levels of self-awareness. In fact, Enneagram teaches that each personality type (or Enneagram number) will have a behavioral shift during times of stress and during times of growth. These shifts are so profound at times, that, depending on circumstances in your life, it may appear that your personality type changes!

Wing Number

The numbers on either side of your number are your wing numbers. Most of us lean toward one of these two numbers and pick up some of its characteristics. We are also able to swing back and forth like a pendulum between these two numbers, channeling the traits and energy from each as we need them. As a result, two people with the same primary Enneagram type can appear completely different.

For example, a Type 6 with a 5-wing tends to be serious and focused. They are hard-working, thoughtful, cautious, and independent, as well as very loyal to those they support. Whereas a Type 6 with a 7-wing will be more engaging and personable in their behavior. They are much more sociable than other Type 6s and love to make new friends.

Stress and Security Numbers

In life, it is a rare occurrence when we are just completely "neutral" in our own lives. As such, I always envision this aspect of Enneagram as if I am on the old-school playground equipment known as a teeter-totter or seesaw. Do you remember how hard it was to get that thing to balance perfectly in the middle? I do, and it rarely happened to me! So, too, is it rare that you are in a place of complete neutrality without positive stress (eustress) or negative stress (distress).

The truth is that our lives are in constant flux. Some days we are up, and some days we are down. We all intuitively understand this. However, the power of Enneagram puts a tool in your hands to help you better understand why and how our behaviors shift under stress so that we can begin to operate based on our desired outcomes instead of off our default personality predispositions.

Our personalities are connected to two other numbers on the Enneagram wheel by arrows (refer to the Enneagram wheel image earlier in the chapter). One arrow (broken) points toward another number from yours.

As a point of clarity, some Enneagram resources define the process of moving from stress to neutral to security as integration or growth (toward security) and disintegration (toward stress).

This is your Stress number. When you are stressed, overtaxed, or under fire, your personality moves toward the more negative traits of your stress number.

- Type 1s, who are typically methodical, become moody and less rational, like Type 4.
- Type 2s, who are typically thoughtful and empathetic, become aggressive and domineering like Type 8.
- Type 3s, who are typically hyper-driven, become disengaged and apathetic, like Type 9.
- Type 4s, who are typically aloof and artistic, become over-involved and clingy, like Type 2.
- Type 5s, who are typically detached and lost in their own thoughts, become hyperactive and scattered like Type 7.
- Type 6s, who are dutiful and committed, become competitive and arrogant, like Type 3.
- Type 7s, who are scattered and whimsical, become perfectionistic and critical, like Type 1.
- Type 8s, who are self-confident and assertive, become secretive and reclusive, like Type 5.
- Type 9s, who are constantly seeking peace and avoiding conflict, become anxious and worried, like Type 6.

The other arrow (solid) points back *from* another number. This is your Security number. When you are happy, fulfilled, or in flow, your personality moves toward the more positive traits of your security number.

- Type 1s, who can be angry and critical, become spontaneous and full of joy like Type 7.
- Type 2s, who can be prideful and clingy, become more self-nurturing and emotionally aware, like Type 4.

- Type 3s, who can be vain and competitive, become cooperative and committed to others, like Type 6.
- Type 4s, who can be jealous and emotionally erratic, become more objective and principled, like Type 1.
- Type 5s, who can be reclusive and doubt their own personal significance, become self-confident and decisive, like Type 8.
- Type 6s, who can be fearful and pessimistic, become more relaxed and optimistic, like Type 9.
- Type 7s, who can be gluttonous and scattered, become more focused and profound, like Type 5.
- Type 8s, who can be intense and controlling, become more open-hearted and empathetic, like Type 2.
- Type 9s, who can be slothful and self-neglecting, become more energetic and ambitious, like Type 3.

While movement toward security is an undoubted goal of each type, it is not as simple as it may seem. Conscious and rational choice is needed, in many cases, to move more frequently toward your security number; however, it is not accomplished by imitating the attitudes and behaviors of that personality type. In order to move toward your area of integration or security, you must actually *let go* of your natural predispositions and instinctive behavioral reactions, rather than imitate the characteristics of some other type.

Moving toward your security number is about owning the characteristics within your personality type that block you, and identifying your defenses, fears, and attitudes that limit you. By doing so, we naturally move toward our number of growth, security, or integration.

A profound advantage of the Enneagram is that once you become aware of how you change in response to stress and security—the negative qualities of your stress number and the positive qualities of your security number—you can catch yourself sliding into disintegration and make better choices than you have in the past.

CHAPTER I

Personally, this understanding has had a profound impact on my professional success and my performance as a husband and father. After becoming more versed in Enneagram, I learned that as a Type 8, I could become more reclusive under stress. Only then did I realize that a telltale sign indicating I was under stress was when I started to shut my door frequently at work.

Typically, I work with the door open, but when I am under significant stress I tend to keep my office door closed when I am working. I've noticed that this usually starts a few days before other undesirable traits of my personality emerge. Understanding the what and why behind this simple behavior, which I would have never noticed without Enneagram, is significant and has been a game changer. Now, I perform "early intervention" and do the internal work necessary to move back toward security and healthy behaviors well before I would have ever noticed prior to doing this work. Pointedly, it has helped me from self-sabotaging myself at work and home. As my mentor has told me time and time again, "Who we are determines how well what we do works."

Chapter 2

Tips on How to Use This Book

On a cold bus ride home from a wrestling tournament during my freshman year of high school, our coach told us that our team was so uncompetitive that the tournament organizer was considering not inviting us back the following year. With a smirk on his face, he spoke these sad words in a clearly self-defeating manner.

I was frustrated beyond belief, but the tournament organizer was right. We only had ten guys on the team, and we were terrible. For reference, there are fourteen weight classes in wrestling. This meant that not only did we not have any depth but also we had four weight classes that we would never compete in during the season. Moreover, of the ten athletes on the team, seven were freshmen.

Word trickled into the school shortly after the season that we would be getting a new coach. Everyone knew it was time for a change. The new coach came with a reputation for turning around struggling programs, and, man, did we fit the bill. As the season approached, we heard more about this coach and our excitement only grew. We believed this was our chance to turn around the program.

Our excitement quickly faded as soon as the first practice started. Coach walked in and everything changed. We were used to the laid-back, easy practices from the year before. This new coach was not laid back, and nothing about his practice was easy.

He set the tone right away. His team rules were straightforward and demanding, and addressed every conceivable detail. His interactions with every single athlete in practice and at meets were straightforward and demanding. His interactions with our parents, administration, and the press were straightforward and demanding.

To be clear, Coach was not mean. He did not try to intimidate anyone. He was just a no-nonsense guy who knew the sport and knew himself. He was consistent. He was aware. He was a great coach.

Still, it was his first year and we were not fully sure how we felt about him as his team. That all changed one day about two months into the long winter athletic season. Coach was late for practice because his car broke down, and his rule was that if you were late to practice—even ten seconds late, as he would often remind us—you had to run stairs for thirty minutes after practice. On that cold January day, after we finished a tough practice and had gathered our things from the locker room, we walked back into the gym and were stunned to see him running up and down the stairs as we walked out.

He demanded accountability from us, but he reciprocated it tenfold. He was the first coach I ever had that took responsibility for telling me to do the wrong thing during a match, or for not preparing our team properly for a meet. He modeled everything he wanted us to be.

He held himself to the same standard he held us to. At that moment, when we walked out of the locker room and saw him running stairs, he officially had us. We were his team. We were ready to be the athletes that helped turn his program around. He had gained our trust. He had our trust because everything about him was consistent. The way he acted in practice, at meets, and in the hallways at school was exactly the same, and we knew what we would get from him.

He was authentic. He was not charismatic. He never gave a great pre-match speech. He was short on affirmations and quick to call out negative behaviors. However, he was unabashedly passionate about the sport and his athletes.

And, as a result, we started to win. By the time I was a senior, we won that same tournament that we were threatened to get kicked out of just three years earlier. To say posing for that team photograph with the trophy felt amazing is an understatement. At that point, we were a perennial power in the area. Just two years after I graduated, our team won the state championship. The turnaround was complete.

The moral of this story is that our success as a team had little to do with his drills or practice routine. Coaches all over the state and country ran the same drills. It was not about *what* he did; it was about *how* he did it.

He was always the same. Win or lose, November or March, in front of the principal or alone in the locker room, his attitude and behaviors never changed. There was absolute clarity in what he was going to demand from his athletes, and absolute clarity in what he was going to give to his athletes, as well. He was truly authentic, and that generated our trust. He leveraged this trust to push us beyond what we thought we were capable of, and, as a result, we continued to improve.

What's Next

In the subsequent chapters, we will provide detailed explanations of each Enneagram type and how each type may react as a coach or an athlete in competitive situations. As we move on to doing so, it is imperative that we reiterate why we are writing this book. This book is about creating the best version of you, not creating a new you.

Invariably, as we move through the nine types, many readers will come to the conclusion that their type is a handicap and holds them back from achieving their dreams. "If I'm going to be successful, I'm going to have to become a Type 8," or whatever number they feel would make it easier for them to succeed. Nothing is further from the truth. Your personality is your superpower, but it is also your Achilles' heel. This book is designed to help you leverage what is already inside of you, not to change you into something new.

If you are still thinking that you would like to be a different Enneagram type or if you feel that way as you read the subsequent chapters—please do yourself a favor and stop. The problem with this line of thinking is twofold.

One, you can't change who you are. A tiger cannot change its stripes. This is not just our opinion—it is something that has been studied for decades. Your personality, for most people, is predominantly formed early in your elementary years.

To be clear, there are many studies from highly reputable universities and organizations that may speak to the fact that personalities can change throughout the entire course of your life. We agree that behavioral tendencies and characteristics can and *should* continue to evolve throughout your life. That, however, is not what we mean by your personality.

In this book, we define personality as your default or autopilot reaction based on your basic desires and basic fears. Thus, what we are contending (and research supports) is that many of the personality traits and characteristics found as early as first grade will persist throughout your life (Nave C. S., Sherman R. A., Funder D. C., Hampson S. E., Goldberg L. R. "On the Contextual Independence of Personality: Teachers' Assessments Predict Directly Observed Behavior after Four Decades." [*Soc Psychol Personal Sci.* 2010 Jul 8; 3(1):1–9. PMID: 20890402; PMCID: PMC2947027]).

To repeat our earlier point, this is not a bad thing!

What this means is that our default is our default. We can, and should, continue to mature, and our behaviors should continue to transform as we continue our journey throughout life. As much as we mature, however, we will still have the same personality that we default to when we are on autopilot.

Trying to fight against this wastes a lot of energy and valuable time.

Second, believe us when we say that there is no ideal formula or personality necessary to be a great coach. As an example, consider all-time great coaches in the same sport and see if you notice more similarities or differences. For basketball, consider Pat Riley, Pat Summitt, Roy Williams, C. Vivian Stringer, and Phil Jackson. For football, think Bill Belichek, Mike Tomlin, Nick Saban, Tony Dungy, and Andy Reid.

Clearly, in the example provided of basketball coaches, Pat Riley and Phil Jackson are foils of each other, and the other coaches probably fall somewhere in between. The same conclusion can be drawn by looking at the football coaches. This list could go on and on with examples of other coaches in other sports, but, hopefully, you are starting to really understand that there is no "right" or ideal personality type in order to be wildly successful.

The value that you bring is that you are you! When studying great coaches from every walk of life, like we did in order to best write this book, you will find one common trait in each of them. They are all authentic. One of our favorite quotes about authenticity and self-awareness, is "I bring all of me wherever I go." To us, this means that understanding exactly who we are, amazing traits and default mechanisms we are not fond of alike, contributes directly to our level of success.

Authenticity is a popular education, leadership, and business buzzword right now, but it truly is the secret sauce that separates good coaches from great ones. Authenticity is the degree to which a person's actions are consistent with his beliefs, values, and desires, despite external pressures (Rich Diviney, *The Attributes* [New York: Random House, 2021]).

Authenticity manifests by being consistent in your thoughts, words, and deeds. *Authenticity means you behave as you believe.* Values guide your interactions at every level. It is being the same person at home, with your friends, and with your boss, as you are on the court, on the field, or in the classroom. Authentic coaches and leaders demonstrate incredibly high character because who they are in private is the same as who they are in public.

Unsuccessful coaches and leaders often are imitating what they see as successful. They are trying to find the formula to be successful. They are in search of the next autobiography or clinic that will show them the way. While every learning experience is worthwhile, there is no one specific formula to follow.

You must be you—no matter what. The point of this book is to help you be the best possible version of yourself that you can be.

Think back through all the coaches that had a significant impact on your life. Why were they able to get you to do the things that you thought you couldn't? Why did you follow their every word even if you didn't understand how it would help? How were they able to get you and your teammates to come together and follow their game plan?

In a word: trust.

However, trust is not something that a coach can demand. It is something that has to be earned, and it is earned through consistency and transparency. Trust is earned when your actions match your words to the point that you become predictable by those that know you best. Trust is dependent upon authenticity.

> *"Trust is developed through open and honest communication and, once established, creates a shared vision for a common goal. Established trust among a group of individuals bolsters a feeling of confidence that only comes in knowing that you are not alone."* –Coach K

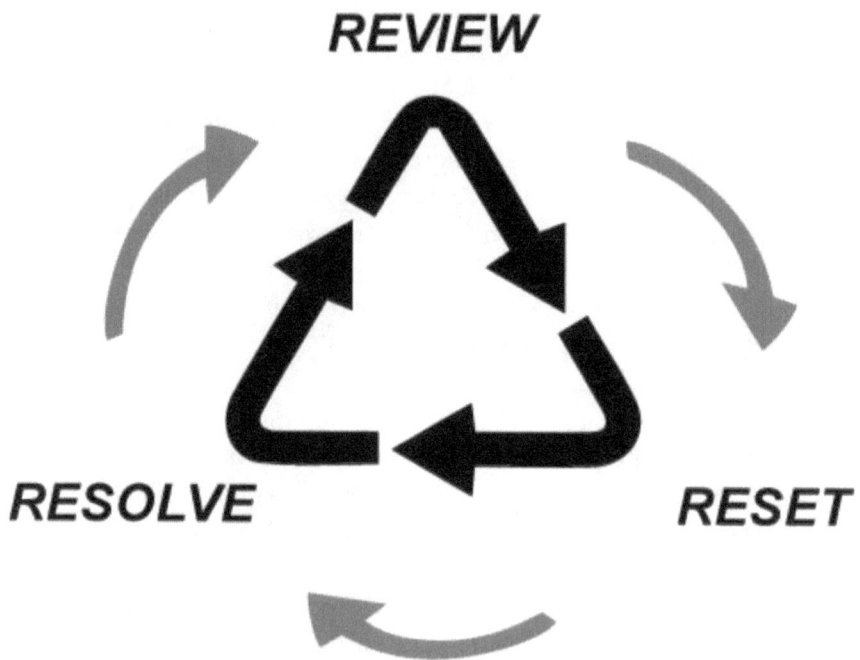

REVIEW - RESET - RESOLVE
The purpose of this book is to help you discover who you are so you can become the best version of yourself. It is to show you your strengths that you can lean on during challenging times and to help identify how your personality will throw up roadblocks that make it harder to turn things around. You can't change who you are, but you can absolutely create the best version of yourself and change your behaviors.

The three-step process you will see referred to throughout the book that we hope you will start to deploy is: Review – Reset – Resolve. We will refer to this as "R^3" in shorthand. While a simple three-step process may seem easy, it will certainly take diligent effort to deploy this strategy.

Review

In order to review a situation or circumstance, you must be fully present in the moment. You must cue in your senses to ensure that you are aware of the circumstances happening around you, individuals' reactions to those circumstances, the collective response to the situation, and your personal instinctive response. If you recall, in the introduction, we referred to the different key types of awareness: self, team, and, ultimately, situational awareness. In order to review the situation, you must remain aware of all four of these contexts. The tough part is that this has to happen in real time. The challenge is to have the discipline to take the millisecond necessary to review all this information and to understand your instinctive behavioral response.

Reset

This is the easy part. Maybe. To reset, do nothing except take inventory of the situation and *choose* your desired response. The key here is that you are not reacting or on autopilot. You take ownership of the situation and deploy the response you find necessary to achieve the results that you desire. This one-second pause between the event and your ultimate response is, oftentimes, the difference between success and failure.

Resolve

Once you have identified the best behavior for you to exhibit to get the response you desire, go after it. It is imperative that you commit fully to this behavior and see it through. I understand that some of you reading this right now might be asking, "If I am choosing my behavior based on each situation, how can that demonstrate authenticity?" Authenticity comes from matching your behavior to your beliefs and values over and over again, consistently. The behaviors may change—the beliefs and values that drive the behavior must stay consistent.

Chapter 2

The R^3 method is something you already do. All great coaches either innately know this or have learned it. The problem is that you probably execute it well only occasionally. After reading this book, you'll have all the tools you need to do it consistently.

Chapter 3

Type 1 Deep Dive

Coach Andrea Kiely took over a disaster of a soccer program. During the prior year, the varsity coach was terminated mid-year for, among other things, leaving an injured player at an opposing team's field because she was no longer of use to the team. The program needed a complete overhaul and facelift. That is where Coach Kiely came in.

Andrea was a science teacher in the school she would be coaching for, and, as an alumnus, had played soccer for the program. It seemed the perfect scenario; however, Andrea had been a player on the team only five years earlier.

Andrea wanted to restore the pride of the program but also knew that discipline may be difficult, given her age and proximity to the players. At the very first player meeting, Coach Kiely announced that any player who received a yellow card would be benched for the remainder of the game—no exceptions.

Coach Kiely's transition was made more complicated by the fact that the team had two star players. This is normally a good thing, but not necessarily so when the two are seemingly always at odds. Shortly after the start of the season, the struggle between the two culminated around the topic of yellow cards.

Sarah was a senior and an incredibly gifted soccer player. She was bold. She was daring. However, all the things that made her great also led to her racking up seven—yes, seven—yellow cards during her junior season. Coach's early season proclamation concerning the consequence of earning yellow cards was all but directed at Sarah.

Chapter 3

Janey was a sophomore and was clearly going to be a star. Janey was typically mild-mannered and easy to coach. If Andrea said to do something a particular way, Janey complied, never questioning her coach. In fact, the only time Janey ever spoke up was if someone was violating the rules or cutting corners.

The first conference game of the season was against an overmatched team from two counties to the west, and it was clear from the beginning that their strategy was to "flop" whenever any contact was made. Three times in the first half this technique was deployed and stopped scoring chances for Coach Kiely's team. The game started to grow contentious, and the fans were at a fever pitch.

Then, with the game still tied 0–0 late in the first half, Janey broke away from the pack with one defender to beat. As Janey entered the box and prepared to shoot, the defender made shoulder-to-shoulder contact with her (legal) as Janey prepared to shoot. Undeterred, Janey buried the ball in the top left corner to, seemingly, give her team a 1–0 lead.

The whistle blew, however, and due to the flop by the defender, Janey was called for pushing off, and the goal was disallowed. Janey, typically quiet, yelled, "THAT'S NOT FAIR!" three consecutive times, and was issued a yellow card.

Janey joined Coach Kiely on the bench and stayed there throughout the entirety of the second half, watching as the game would eventually end in a 1–1 tie. Two weeks later, Coach Kiely's team was playing the top-rated team in the region amid a windstorm. This storm was blowing directly south on a north-south-facing field. During the first half, Janey and Sarah's team was forced to play against the wind; they moved the ball into the other team's box only once and were eventually awarded a penalty kick to miraculously take a 1–0 lead.

With two minutes left in the half, the score remained the same. Sarah gained control of the ball and began to stall. Clearly, she was hoping to go into halftime leading and emerge with the wind at their backs for the second half. She dribbled it to the corner, was challenged, and skillfully played it off her opponent. She then took a very long time to throw the ball into play. It was returned to her and she did the same thing again.

Shockingly, the official levied a yellow card for stalling/"delay of game" on Sarah. This call was controversial, but a yellow card is a yellow card, and now Sarah was in violation of Coach Kiely's rule.

Except, this time Coach did not bench Sarah. She had decided that the intent of the rule was to stop aggressive physical contact with the other team and to prevent her team from interacting with the officials. This yellow card did not meet the *spirit* of the rule, so she allowed Sarah to return to action in the second half.

Nobody seemed to take issue with the decision, except Janey. Coach Kiely decided Janey's subsequent disconnection from her as a coach was simply petulant jealousy of Sarah, who was the senior captain. Coach Kiely learned this was certainly not the case after she took the time to understand that Janey was an Enneagram Type 1.

Description of Enneagram Type 1

An Enneagram Type 1 is frequently called "the Perfectionist." They are principled, ethical, idealistic, and have a strong sense of right and wrong. Type 1s perceive the world as rife with errors and imperfections and feel compelled to correct it. They are typically great teachers and advocates for change. Perfectionists believe they must be good and right in order to deserve love, adulation, and praise. As a result, Type 1s are thoughtful, responsible, improvement-oriented, and self-controlled. However, this often leads them to be critical, resentful, and self-judging.

Type 1s' minds are naturally drawn to spot problems, and, as a result, they are constantly trying to improve things—both tangible and intangible. This perception can lead them to be excellent problem solvers and invaluable system creators; unfortunately, this compulsion to "fix" the world around them can drive them to fixate on all the ills and broken rules they see, leading them to be very judgmental and resentful of the people closest to them. The arbitrary and autocratic assertions of right and wrong lead Type 1s to often come across as condescending, since in their minds, what is self-evident to them should also be self-evident to everyone else.

Chapter 3

Triad

As part of the Anger Triad, Type 1s internalize their anger in the form of deep-seething resentment for all the "rule breakers" they see around them. Type 1s believe the world judges—or perhaps, more accurately, should judge—those who don't follow the rules, control their emotions, or behave appropriately.

However, all they see is a world full of people having a great time indulging in their desires, breaking the rules, and not getting "caught"—hence, the resentment. When externalized, this resentment can be expressed as obsessive-compulsive micromanaging of those around them. This inflexible and dogmatic behavior causes Type 1s to appear cold and insensitive.

This resentment is not only reserved for others; this Enneagram type may be best understood as having an intense and relentless inner critic. In fact, the judgment that they display outwardly pales in comparison to the judgment of their own internal critic.

Comparison to other Types in the Anger/Gut Triad

Anger for this triad can be compared to acid. Type 8s want to get the acid out as soon as possible, and Type 9s want to forget about, or hide, the acid until eventually it builds up inside and explodes. Type 1s hold on to the acid as it burns inside of them as resentment.

Motivations

Enneagram Type 1s are motivated by the desire to live "the right way," to make sure everyone else lives "the right way," and to improve the world around them. The high standards they place on not only themselves but also others lead to a compulsive need to perfect the world and to repress impulses and desire for pleasure. Their behaviors, when on autopilot, usually lead Type 1s to be very opinionated, which can show up as constantly correcting people and badgering them to do things "the right way." The "right way," more often than not, is defined only by them with no input from coaches or teammates.

Fear

The basic fear of Type 1s is being corrupt or evil, and even more so, others recognizing this imperfection, then receiving fault or blame. Because of this fear, Type 1s work tirelessly to ensure that they are above reproach and that no one can rightfully criticize them. As a result, it is often hard for a Type 1 to relax or have fun out of the fear that something might go wrong on their watch and it will be all their fault—or even worse, if that something went wrong because they gave into their unsavory impulses. This constant pressure, and the projection of their ridiculously high standards on others, tends to alienate Type 1s who seemingly choose alone over imperfect.

Craving

Type 1s crave perfection. This craving can be an invaluable tool when tempered. Type 1s can create systems and rules that turn teams, organizations, schools, or businesses into well-oiled machines. This craving for perfection often forces a Type 1 to focus much more on the process than on people, though. As a result of humans being a part of each system, perfection is not attainable. There will always be something or someone that needs improvement. Constantly craving perfection leads to disproportionate levels of overwork, burnout, and depression for Type 1s and those that they are in charge of.

Self-Sabotage

The motivation, fear, and craving of the Enneagram Type 1 manifest in self-sabotaging behaviors when they operate on autopilot and destroy progress in the pursuit of perfection. The pursuit of perfection can be healthy as long as one understands that it is not attainable. This is an important distinction for not only Type 1s as individuals but also for those with whom they interact. As a coach, leader, or member of a team, a Type 1 on autopilot can create disharmony because their default drive for perfection demonstrates little value or appreciation for the progress made along the way. Small celebrations and short rests during this pursuit of perfection will help avoid self-sabotage for Type 1s.

CHAPTER 3

Role on a Team

Type 1s are typically part of the leadership team, if not necessarily the established and titled leader. Typically, Type 1s fare much better as the second-in-command. The fear of making a mistake can lead to an inability to make decisions, thus leading to ineffectiveness in leadership roles for a Type 1. However, as the "number two," they can be excellent executors of the leader's plan due to their incredible work ethic and ability to create systems. Additionally, Type 1s function very well in risk management roles, and ensure teams and organizations abide by legal, moral, and ethical mandates.

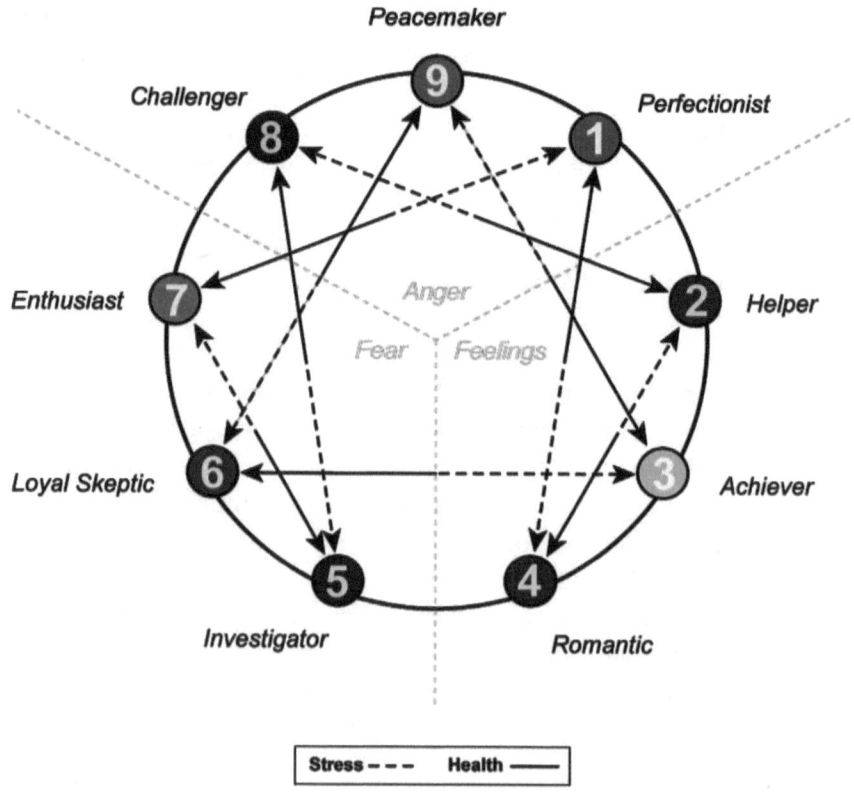

Type 1 Deep Dive

Continuum of Behaviors
Every Enneagram type has default behaviors but also a predisposition to behave in different ways depending upon their emotional and behavioral health. When healthy, Type 1s behave like Enneagram Type 7s; and when under stress, they typically behave like Enneagram Type 4s.

Healthy

Type 1s, who can be judgmental and rigid become more spontaneous and fun, like Type 7s.

Stress

Type 1s, who are conscientious and ethical, become depressed and moody, like Type 4s.

Same, But Different—Enneagram Wings
Although there are nine basic personality types in the Enneagram, each type can be influenced by the types on either side, making two people of the same Enneagram type appear very different. In the case of Type 1s, they can either lean toward Type 2 or Type 9.

Type 1s with a 2-wing are more extroverted and empathetic and typically act as an advocate for other people. This advocate role, however, can come off as controlling or critical of others in order to help them become the best version of themselves. In this scenario, it is common for a Type 1 to come across as condescending because they simultaneously want to advocate for others, and want to feel appreciated.

Type 1s with a 9-wing are more introverted, detached, and easygoing. They still possess a strong sense of right and wrong but are more open to new ideas and different perspectives. They are much less black and white. Their outward laid-back demeanor makes it easier for these Type 1s to build and maintain relationships.

I might be an Enneagram Type 1 if . . .
- I tend to see only the mistakes and flaws in the world around me.
- I feel like it is my place to correct others when I see or hear them make mistakes.

- I feel like I try much harder than others to do things correctly.
- I lose all trust in someone if I believe they are implementing rules or procedures unfairly or unjustly.
- I get lost in the details looking to see how I can make something better.
- I become angry when I see others ignore or break the rules.
- I find myself continually being overly critical and judgmental of others.
- I have a lot of self-discipline but despise the fact that I have impulses that require such discipline, and can't figure out why others don't have self-discipline.
- I see the world as black and white.
- I can't shut it down and relax because I just have too much work that needs to get done.
- I wish others would work as hard as I do so I wouldn't constantly have to redo their work.
- I feel like I can't forgive someone because they should be punished for making a mistake that hurt me.

R^3

Coach Morris was an elite athlete. He came from an incredible pedigree as a high school All-American and Division I athlete. Though Coach Morris was a swimmer and he coaches volleyball, a circumstance we see frequently with highly successful coaches, the issue is that his entire background and context for how to coach the sport "the right way" came from his mentor, Coach Timm.

Coach Timm was a legendary volleyball coach who led a program at a large high school for over two decades. He was rough around the edges and demanding. In fact, each year for tryouts he would set up trash buckets around the court because he expected his athletes to vomit. In some cases, he would mandate vomiting from conditioning drills before practice would start.

Somehow, his old-school practices were essentially grandfathered in as acceptable to the community. Sure, he lost some athletes along the way, but the high school was so large, and club volleyball was so prominent in the area, that he had plenty of athletes at his disposal should some decide to quit.

This was the tutelage Coach Morris learned under. This extreme mentality and training were not foreign to him because of the individual rigors of training for swimming. Swimmers are among the most conditioned athletes in the world. Thus, Coach Timm's practices did not offend his sensibilities. Moreover, when athletes quit, Coach Morris was quick to blame the athlete for not adhering to the rules and guidelines of what it meant to be a Julian High School volleyball player.

Coach Timm retired, and Coach Morris had his first head coaching position. He ran an almost identical program to Coach Timm, but somehow the behavior from Coach Morris was less tolerated than it was from his predecessor. As the pushback became increasingly pronounced, Coach Morris decided that the Julian volleyball community had grown "soft" and sought a coaching position elsewhere.

As an experienced coach and decorated athlete, it was not hard for Coach Morris to find another position just weeks after leaving Julian. He was excited to get to work, and during summer conditioning, he continued to be a full-blown disciple of Coach Timm and instituted an extreme training regimen.

Unlike at Julian, there was not a large outcry from the community or groundswell that caused the school administration to take notice. Instead, the sheer data made his coaching style an immediate topic of conversation. There were thirty-seven girls on the opening day of conditioning, but by the time the fall volleyball season rolled around, there were only sixteen girls left in the entire program. People did not complain with their voices or on social media; people complained with their lack of participation.

The athletic director sat Coach Morris down and explained the situation to him. He encouraged him to reconsider his training methodology and to re-recruit some of the athletes who chose not to try out. Coach Morris rejected that idea emphatically, noting that doing so is not the right way to build a program. The athletic director agreed to disagree with Coach Morris, and gave him a year to figure things out to build the numbers back.

Coach Morris did not change. In fact, he doubled down on his measures in an effort to build team chemistry and foundational values for the organization. By the end of the season, the team's record was abysmal, and there were eleven girls left standing in the program.

Coach Morris was relieved of his duties shortly after the conclusion of the season.

Here is how Coach Morris might have handled the situation if he had a better understanding of himself and had used the R^3 method.

Review

If Coach Morris would have reviewed the situation through a lens of self-understanding, he would have understood that he was operating on autopilot. As an Enneagram Type 1, he was compelled to act primarily out of a sense of right and wrong. While he believed his methodology was correct because that was the way he had been taught, if he would have taken a moment to reset, he may have viewed the situation from a more objective perspective.

Reset

In this scenario, Coach Morris had the perfect opportunity to reset. He had a mentor or coach that cared enough about him to sit him down and alert him to the potential downside of his behavior. Instead of taking this time to reset, Coach Morris doubled down. This may happen more often for Type 1s than other types because they believe they are operating out of a fundamental virtue.

Resolve

The resolution in this scenario would have been Coach Morris being less consumed with being right, and more concerned with creating the outcomes he desired for his athletes and his program. Specifically, in this circumstance, he would have dialed back the intensity of training, questioned his methods, and re-recruited the athletes that had quit the program.

Type 1s can be an amazing asset to any organization, and we have worked with some incredible Type 1 coaches and leaders. However, the desire to seek perfection and aim to be right can be a blinding compulsion for Type 1s. Oftentimes, when coaching a Type 1 we are forced to ask whether they would rather be right or rather be effective. In this situation, if Coach Morris backed off on the training he would have retained or recruited more athletes. However, he saw that as not doing things the right way and was willing to ultimately sacrifice his job instead of looking inward to increase his self-awareness and create better outcomes for the program and his athletes.

Tomorrow Takeaways

- Carry a journal with you for a day and write down everything your internal critic says.
    - Take note of how often you criticize yourself, what things you are most critical of, and what language your "internal critic" uses.
    - Identify the areas of your life (or sport) where the critic is the loudest and discuss this with a coach, mentor, or loved one.
- Use the information recorded in your journal to analyze how much this voice interferes with your decisiveness and causes you to procrastinate.
- Analyze how your constant criticism and judgment stifles the joy of the game for you, your players, and your coaches. To extend this, do the same exercise from the perspective of your family and friends—this part may be painful.
- What aspects of your life would be improved if you would allow yourself to make mistakes? What would happen to your level of creativity? Your level of decisiveness?

- Discuss with your players and coaches what you can let go of, without judgment or redoing their work, that would make your team perform better. Ideas include:
  - Practice schedule
  - Play-calling
  - Warm-up routine
  - Community outreach
  - Social media
- Conduct the same exercise asking them what they can let go of to find liberation and the joy of the game again.

Chapter 4

Type 2 Deep Dive

Coach Sarah Craig was entering her fourteenth year as the women's basketball coach at the high school she taught at just outside of Denver. Coach Craig was as successful and well-liked as any coach in the athletic program at Lincolnbrook High School. One of the reasons Coach Craig was well-liked was her refusal to stay stagnant. She was always bringing some new ideas to the program and keeping it fresh.

During the off-season, Coach Craig had read much about student-led programs and was interested in trying this strategy out. Since Coach Craig's first season, she had always established an annual theme that would help to define the season. As she thought through how to make her program more student-led, she decided that allowing the varsity players to determine the theme for the year was the perfect introduction to this coaching philosophy.

Two weeks prior to the start of the season, Coach Craig called a mandatory meeting in which she outlined the expectations for the season. This is a version of the same meeting that every coach around the country has every year. The change was at the end of this meeting, Coach Craig issued the challenge to the upperclassmen to come to her the day before the first try-out and share what the consensus theme for the year would be.

The girls were very excited about this and immediately started a group chat to start debating ideas. The first few days were full of ideas being tossed around, but after the first weekend with this being the topic of the group chat, two themes emerged as de facto finalists: "selfless" and "finish."

"Selfless" was suggested by Pamela, who was going to be their three-year starting point guard this upcoming season. "Finish" was brought forward by Trina, who was going to be their three-year starting forward this upcoming season—and their only Division I recruit in the program. Pamela and Trina were seemingly best friends on the court but, given the large size of Lincolnbrook, did not seem to be in the same friend group outside of basketball.

Trina adhered strongly to the theme "finish" since they were up twelve points in the second half of the Regional Championship game the year prior and let it slip away. Likewise, Pamela held strong to "selfless" since the reason the game slipped away is that everyone tried to win the game themselves. The group chat continued until there were only two days left to tell Coach Craig what the theme would be, and there was still no consensus.

The two team leaders, and strongest advocates of the finalist themes, grew frustrated with the group chat and decided to meet for ice cream to discuss because some of the comments on the chat had grown petty and they did not want to start the season that way. Trina was firmly committed to her theme upon entering the conversation that day, but seeing how focused Pamela was on this dramatically changed her mind. Trina thought to herself of how Pamela was always serving everyone else, and if she felt this strongly about the theme, then she could have this.

The two ended the ice cream meeting laughing and excited about the year with the theme of "selfless." Coach Craig instantly approved of the theme, made t-shirts, and made being selfless either the prominent or underlying theme of every drill, every practice, and every scrimmage headed into the regular season.

Lincolnbrook started the season off on fire! While Lincolnbrook had aspirations of winning the Regional Championship, nobody was talking about them making a deep state title run. That was, until early January, when Lincolnbrook had rattled off seventeen straight victories, including multiple wins over state-ranked teams. People took notice. Moreover, Pamela and Trina were both playing at all-state levels. Pamela was the ultimate facilitator averaging less than ten points a game, but over ten assists, and always positioned to guard the other team's best player. On average, more than five of Pamela's assists per game were made directly to Trina. And Trina was doing what she always did—scoring the points. She was averaging over twenty-five points per game. This was just one of those years that felt like there was a little magic to it.

This led up to their biggest game of the year. Ironically, at the beginning of the year, nobody thought the game against Valley Glen would be a big game because Valley Glen was the defending state champion with all their starters returning. In November, the girls would have told anyone who asked that this game was going to be a beat down, but now the game was getting regional news coverage. It was the game of the week.

Lincolnbrook went out and executed the way they had all season. Pamela was in complete control of the game and found Trina in all the right spots throughout the first half. Lincolnbrook held a three-point lead entering the second quarter, and Pamela ended the first half with zero points, eleven assists, and three steals. She was playing incredibly well.

The second half was more of the same. Lincolnbrook and Valley Glen were trading amazing play after amazing play. Both teams showed heart, resilience, and talent. With thirteen seconds to go, the game was tied and it was Lincolnbrook's ball. Coach Craig called a timeout. In a surprise move, the inbounds pass was not drawn up to have Pamela create and find the open player. Instead, the play was drawn up for Trina to receive the inbounds pass and to go 1:1 with her woman in isolation to attempt to get the game-winning shot off.

Trina dribbled the ball outside the three-point line until the clock hit four seconds, and she made a quick dribble to her right with a jab step. The defender moved quickly to slide in front of her. Trina then crossed her defender and took two dribbles with her left hand ending up just to the left of the free throw line where she let a sixteen-foot jump shot fly . . . nothing but net!

The team celebrated. Coach Craig, having managed personalities before, watched closely to see if Pamela had any initial reaction to not getting the ball on the final play. She was relieved to see that Pamela was the first to playfully tackle Trina after the ball went through the net. Coach Craig thought to herself that this may be a truly special season.

Given that multiple news stations were covering the game, there were many interview requests. Strangely, none of them came for Pamela, who ended the game with only four points, but nineteen assists—a school record. Pamela took notice, but went into the locker room and celebrated with the team. Pamela hurried home to check out the news coverage of the game to make sure the highlights were recorded.

Pamela watched with interest as Coach Craig and Trina were interviewed on all three of the local stations. She couldn't help but notice that in three interviews given by the two women, Pamela and her record-setting game were not mentioned once. The focus was on the game-winning shot and Trina's ability to outshine the Division I recruits on the other team.

Pamela was hurt. She was angry. She began to think about how she was both a scorer and passer on her travel teams but gave all of that up to be the ultimate team player, and now nobody was recognizing her. She stewed about it all weekend.

While Pamela did not say anything about the way she was feeling, every time Coach Craig mentioned the theme of "selfless," Pamela's blood began to boil. All she could do was think to herself how selfless it would have been for Coach Craig and Trina to give her a little bit of credit after all she gave to her team, particularly to the two of them.

During the next game, Pamela decided to look for her own shot and for other teammates. If Trina and Coach Craig were so great that they did not need her, then they could find ways to score on their own. The change in the play of the team was noticeable.

This continued without conversation or intervention for over a month as the team began to unravel. Coach Craig continued to preach selflessness, and every time she did, it pushed Pamela further away from the team, until the team was playing so dysfunctionally that they were barely competitive.

Pamela was an Enneagram Type 2 and caught in a very unhealthy cycle that went unmitigated and, without intervention, continued to get worse. While Coach Craig was typically in tune with her team, a deeper understanding of Enneagram, and her players, could have avoided this unfortunate unraveling.

Description of an Enneagram Type 2

An Enneagram Type 2 is often called "the Helper." They are caring, empathetic, friendly, and self-sacrificing. Type 2s have an insatiable desire to help others in any way they can. Type 2s often sacrifice their own needs and wants for the benefit of others. Most people see them as great friends who are always there for them. However, this autopilot behavior of helping and putting others first is (perhaps unknowingly) used as a strategy for earning love and bolstering their self-worth.

Type 2s view the expression of their own feelings and needs as a threat to the health and stability of their relationships until their bottled-up feelings spill over. This can lead to the downside of Type 2s who may appear insecure, prideful, intrusive, demanding, or needy. In the worst circumstances, Type 2s' behavior can become manipulative and controlling, while frequently playing the role of martyr.`

Triad

As part of the Feeling Triad, Type 2s focus outwardly on others' feelings, giving no attention or acknowledgment to their own. The types in this triad are also highly motivated by image, and for Type 2s, the image they are trying to project is that of the ultimate friend and giver in the relationship. However, this image often acts as a facade hiding their true, perhaps even subconscious, intentions.

As stated earlier, Type 2s are helpful and kind as a way to increase their often low self-esteem. In other words, Type 2s do not act altruistically and with kindness out of a sense of purpose to the world. Type 2s do, however, genuinely need and rely on human connection. Unfortunately, often the connection is not authentic as they prove to those they connect with how much the other person needs them. This desire to be needed causes Type 2s to adjust their behavior to their audience, and, at times, this can lead to an appearance of being disingenuous as a result of "shape-shifting" to fit their environments.

Chapter 4

Comparison to Other Types in the Feeling/Heart Triad

Feelings for this triad can be compared to a magnifying glass. Type 3s want to turn the magnifying glass onto themselves so everyone else can get a close-up view of them and they can garner all the attention, and Type 4s want to use the magnifying glass to look at what's inside of them and to investigate what is missing, in hopes they can help reclaim the moment. Type 2s only want to turn the magnifying glass around to focus on everyone else's feelings.

Motivations

Enneagram Type 2s are motivated by the need to be needed and loved, and to avoid acknowledging their own needs. If you ever need help remembering the motivation of a Type 2, remember the song by Cheap Trick "I Want You to Want Me."

Type 2s have an intuitive sense of what others need and have a great capacity for empathy. Upon entering any social interaction, they can instantly spot who needs help and will not hesitate in offering it. Having a high emotional intelligence is the superpower of Type 2s, and nothing is more important to them than their relationships. However, their autopilot behaviors lead to hovering at best, and controlling guilt-mongering at worst, in the form of an "I know what's best for you" attitude.

Fear

The basic fear of a Type 2 is of being unwanted or unloved, or being *unworthy* of love. This fear brings about their diligent quest to make sure everyone is dependent on them by doing everything in their power to help and support others. The basic actions of a Type 2 operating by default can be characterized by the belief that people can't leave you if they can't survive on their own. Thus, their fear is that if they do not do enough for you, they may not be worthy of love, and, consequently, their genuine connection for relationships will be unfulfilled.

Craving

Type 2s want unconditional love and acceptance. In daily behavior, this manifests itself as a desire to be appreciated and acknowledged, because

Type 2s acting on default are not confident that they are worthy of love that they have not earned in some way.

When Type 2s are in a healthy emotional place and this craving is controlled, Type 2s are incredible leaders and teammates. They use their desires for human connection and to be of service to truly help others and become influential leaders or the "glue" that holds teams together. When this craving gets out of control, Type 2s can become overwhelmed from having to be everything to everybody.

Self-Sabotage

The motivation, fear, and craving of the Enneagram Type 2 manifest in self-sabotaging behavior when, operating on autopilot, they do not recognize that they are taking on too much responsibility for others. This invariably ends in overpromising and underdelivering, which undermines relationship trust.

Moreover, this leads to resentment from both those who were overpromised and from the Type 2, who feels underappreciated for at least trying. This drives Type 2s into a cycle of more overpromising and continued mistrust. As a result, the human connection that Type 2s most desire is compromised due to fractured relationships borne out of their default behaviors.

Role on a Team

Type 2s can be found in various roles on most teams. As leaders, Type 2s have an uncanny knack for knowing what a team needs at a given moment. Their natural empathy shines through and they tend to meet the needs of their team quite frequently and with a diverse array of behaviors. Sometimes this may be a fiery motivational talk, other times, a good joke or prank to loosen everyone up, a day off, or even some tough love and accountability.

Regardless of the situation, Type 2s seem to have the emotional quotient (EQ) necessary to pull the right lever. They also make very good teammates and are always trying to put their teammates in a position to receive recognition and accolades. In more athletic terms, they have no problem being the facilitator setting up teammates for the big play.

CHAPTER 4

Continuum of Behaviors

Every Enneagram type has default behaviors but also a predisposition to behave in different ways depending upon their emotional and behavioral health. When healthy, Type 2s behave like Enneagram Type 4s; and when under stress, they typically behave like Enneagram Type 8s.

Healthy

Type 2s, who can, at times, be intrusive and overbearing, become more self-nurturing and empathetic, like a Type 4.

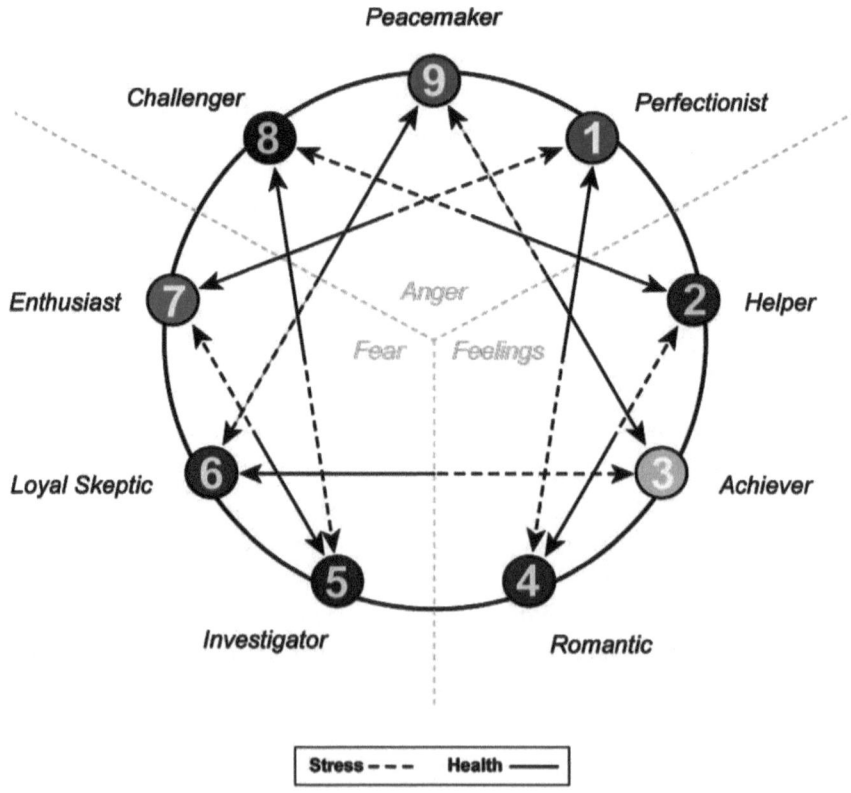

Stress
Type 2s, who are nurturing and encouraging, become aggressive and controlling, like a Type 8.

Same, But Different—Enneagram Wings
Although there are nine basic personality types in the Enneagram, each type can be influenced by the types on either side, making two people of the same Enneagram type appear very different. In the case of Type 2s, they can either lean toward Type 1 or Type 3.

Type 2s with a 1-wing tend to be more dutiful and better at setting boundaries. At best, these people combine the empathy of Type 2 with the moral compass of Type 1, leading many to call this Type/Wing combination the Good Samaritan.

Type 2s with a 3-wing tend to be much more ambitious and confident than their counterparts. While still relationship-driven, the confidence of this type allows for them to also be focused on achievement and the outcomes they desire with less of a direct focus on securing the human connection and relationships which define an archetypical Type 2.

I might be an Enneagram Type 2 if...
- I am often preoccupied with thinking of how I can meet the needs of others.
- I do not feel my love and care is being reciprocated. I guilt other people into acknowledging all I do for them.
- I take pride in giving and helping.
- I sometimes feel that people take advantage of me.
- I find it easier to give than to receive.
- It is easier to be emotionally strong and available for other people than to be emotionally honest with myself.
- I have a hard time expressing my own needs.
- When someone provides more for me than I do for them, I become uncomfortable.
- I can be manipulative and alter how I present myself to others.

- When I am in a bad mood, I go out of my way to make sure others know how much I do for them.
- Sometimes, I will provide support and assistance even if it is not requested. Moreover, sometimes I do so and still resent providing support in the moment.

R^3

Coach Jonathon was a revered coach from a small-town football factory in West Texas oil country. Over his nineteen years as head coach, he brought home three state championships and numerous district titles. He was incredibly competitive and as hard-nosed as they come, which was reflected in his players.

Throughout his successful tenure, two things were constant. Coach Jonathon led the offense, and his assistant, Coach Biggs, ran the defense. Both were extremely innovative and had a knack for understanding their personnel and how to best deploy them. They collaborated plenty, but each had their own area of expertise and led accordingly.

While most years it was Coach Jonathon's wide-open spread offense that got all the attention, it was Coach Biggs's stingy defense that led to their most successful seasons. Said simply, when Coach Biggs had a great year, so did the entire program. This fact was not lost on Coach Jonathon, and he routinely and publicly praised the defense and Coach Biggs after big wins.

Their partnership worked so well for so long because, as Coach Biggs put it, "It doesn't matter who gets the credit, as long as our kids are having fun and winning!" While this was a theory Coach Jonathon also subscribed to, he always thought it was a key part of his job to ensure that he always talked about his other players and coaches more than himself, especially when people outside the program wanted to give him praise. He was almost defiant in ensuring that he made it about someone else, and that someone else was almost always Coach Biggs.

The partnership, however, eventually ended. There was no breakup. Coach Biggs's aching back and knees in need of replacement led him to retirement. Coach Jonathon was as upset that he would not have his friend and confidant around daily as he was concerned about finding a new leader for the defense.

But, as Coach Jonathon headed into his twentieth season, reality was sinking in and he was facing something completely unknown to him: a season without his trusty defensive coordinator and buddy by his side. Knowing the time was coming, Coach Biggs spent his final few seasons grooming his successor so the team could continue its winning ways. Coach Stevens was handpicked by Coach Biggs. He was a young, eager coach, who also happened to be an alumnus that played for Coach Biggs on one of the state championship teams.

Needless to say, everyone felt good about the future of the program.

That season started out like most before it. The team's offense was a juggernaut, putting up points in bunches. However, the defense was struggling, forcing the offense to have to play mistake-free just to win games. While the box scores looked fine, Coach Jonathon knew this was not a sustainable path toward a championship. He also knew that talent-wise, this team had a chance to have that type of season.

This pattern of shootouts and high point totals for both teams continued throughout the season. In storybook fashion, the season came down to the final game against their biggest rival, with a trip to the playoffs on the line for both teams. Win, and you're in. Lose, and the season is over.

Coach Jonathon knew he needed his defense to show up big in this game. As much as he did not want to impact the confidence of Coach Stevens, he felt the boys had worked too hard for him to not pull out every possible trick he had. So he reached out to Coach Biggs to see if he could help Coach Stevens put together a game plan to slow their rivals down and win the game.

Coach Biggs, never one to say no to anyone, happily agreed and spent the week tutoring Coach Stevens on the finer points of coming up with a stifling game plan. Coach Stevens was appreciative but did not flower Coach Biggs in thanks. He was distracted by the game and the clear message that he needed help. He was an attentive student but did not act like an adoring fan.

Chapter 4

Coach Stevens, while perhaps not the warmest he could possibly be to Coach Biggs, apparently listened to every detail of the tutoring he received. As the game unfolded, it became apparent that something was different with the defense. They were flying all over the field and seemed to have an answer for everything thrown at them. As the game ended, a glance at the scoreboard told the whole story: 56–0. It was the first shutout of the year. Heck, it was the first time they had held an opponent under twenty points all year. Coach Stevens, who was previously being bad-mouthed at the local coffee shops, was now the talk of the town.

The first two rounds of the playoffs followed a similar pattern. On Monday, Coach Stevens and Coach Biggs would watch film together. By Tuesday at 5:00 a.m., Coach Stevens would receive an email with some of the finer points to consider beyond what was talked about over film. Coach Stevens never felt more prepared. For the first time all season he was at ease, and the fact that his wife could now go shopping in the area without snide comments was a definite bonus.

The games continued with similar success. The offense was firing on all cylinders, and the defense was suffocating. With Coach Biggs's expert advice, the accolades for Coach Stevens kept pouring in. In the week leading up to the quarterfinals, the local TV channel came in to do a piece about Coach Stevens and his stout defense and their dramatic improvement throughout the course of the year.

The interview aired right before the game, and Coach Stevens did what his head coach had always taught. He tried to push praise away. He gave all the credit to the players' hard work and great play. He noted that the players had been bringing it all year and he was glad they were finally getting the credit they deserved.

The quarterfinal game followed the same script as the previous games, with the defense playing outstandingly. After the game, Coach Stevens called Coach Biggs, as he had done each of the previous games, to revel in their success and to start game planning for the semifinal game. He even planned to tell him that at the Monday film session, he would order in Papa G's, Coach Biggs's favorite pizza place. Straight to voicemail.

He called again the next day with the same outcome. After another call that went straight to voicemail, Coach Stevens asked Coach

Jonathon to check on Coach Biggs and see if everything was all right. Coach Jonathon had a similar string of calls going straight to voicemail. This panicked Coach Jonathon, who eventually got a hold of Coach Biggs's wife. She assured him that everything was fine and that he would call when he was finished in the yard.

Coach Jonathon, relieved that his friend was alright, turned his sights to the next game and forgot about the as-yet-unreturned call from Coach Biggs. He simply assumed he called Coach Stevens back, and their Monday film session would lead to them handling the defensive game plan together.

The semifinal game did not play out like the previous ones. The defense looked off. They looked like a better version of the defense from the beginning of the season. They didn't play terribly but gave up too many big plays. The offense tried to keep up, but in the end, they came up just short.

The end of any season is tough. The bus ride home was eerily quiet though, and the only voices that could be heard were those of Coach Jonathon and Coach Stevens as they talked about the game. Coach Jonathon was stunned to find out that Coach Stevens never did hear back from Coach Biggs—despite calling him a total of thirteen times during the week. Coach Stevens even felt the need to pull out his phone to show Coach Jonathon. Something was off.

Coach Jonathon was dumbfounded. Coach Biggs was always jumping at the chance to help someone. Coach Biggs would even get after Coach Jonathon for being too hard on people at times, and he was always focused on providing people the support they needed. Why would he disappear now? Something was not right.

On his way home, Coach Jonathon stopped at a local restaurant to pick up dinner for his family. He always did this after a loss. It gave him some time to remember that the people at home loved him and that bringing the loss home with him served no good. Almost serendipitously, he saw Coach Biggs walking to his car as he was walking in.

Coach Jonathon smiled to himself and felt relief that he would finally understand what happened. He yelled to his friend from across the parking lot. Coach Biggs stopped, looked at him—perhaps even looked through him, got into his car, and drove off. Coach Jonathon had no idea what was going on.

Coach Jonathon became angry and decided to move on from the situation completely. He intentionally tried not to think of Coach Biggs and eliminated any reference to him around the program and to Coach Stevens. There were no additional attempts to reach out or to find out what the problem was so they could bury the hatchet. Coach Jonathon did a good job of pushing Coach Biggs out of his head until late April when he heard Coach Biggs was being welcomed onto the staff of the biggest rival school, which he had helped shut out just a few short months earlier.

Here is how this situation could have turned out differently had Coach Biggs used the R^3 and had a better understanding of himself.

Review

Coach Biggs acted like a Type 2 who has been hurt. He defaulted to his autopilot behavior of an unhealthy Type 2, which means he was acting like a Type 8. In this case, earlier in the season, Coach Biggs had ridden in as the "hero" to Coach Stevens, Coach Jonathon, the players, and the community. This is exactly the type of role Coach Biggs loves to play.

When all of his help was not rewarded with the recognition (love and admiration) from the coaches, players, or the community, Coach Biggs became resentful. In this case, his resentment led to the passive-aggressive behavior of avoidance to "punish" those that weren't grateful for all his help. Coach Biggs then doubled down on this behavior by pursuing a job opportunity to further demonstrate his worth and his worthiness of praise.

Reset

With this scenario, Coach Biggs had multiple opportunities to reset with all the phone calls he ignored. Through the years of working with Coach Jonathon, he had always gotten the credit and love he craved. In the scenario where he did not, if Coach Biggs had developed a keener level of self-awareness, it would have allowed Coach Biggs to communicate his feelings to Coach Jonathon and Coach Stevens in order to resolve the situation.

Additionally, if Coach Jonathon was more familiar with the Enneagram, he would have known that Coach Biggs needed to be showered with praise by Coach Stevens, just as he was doing for his players. As a coach, his ability to understand those he worked with would have allowed Coach Jonathon to make slightly different decisions—possibly leading to a state championship.

Resolve

Ironically, the quote Coach Biggs used in every interview asking why he never pursued a head coaching job, "It doesn't matter who gets the credit as long as the kids are having fun and we are winning," was the undoing of this championship season. Coach Biggs's own words could have been the resolution to this situation. Had Coach Biggs heeded his own advice, most likely the team would have kept winning. Or, if Coach Jonathon had been aware enough to serve the ego needs of a Type 2 on autopilot, Coach Biggs would have likely been a huge part of the celebration fulfilling his need for recognition.

Type 2s can possess an incredible ability to know just what kind of help people around them need, and are more than willing to provide it. The fee for this help is simply a return of the love and attention that they are giving. As long as this need is met, Type 2s will continue to serve in any capacity they can.

However, if they perceive that their love is not being reciprocated appropriately, the Type 2's fear of being unwanted begins to build. This most often results in passive-aggressiveness at best and lashing out in anger at worst. When working with Type 2s, both parties need to have enough awareness to understand the Type 2's motivation, autopilot behavior, and tendency to devolve into acting like a Type 8 to prevent terminating a relationship.

Tomorrow Takeaways

- Identify how much of your attention is being devoted to other people's needs and analyze how much of that is intentional and thoughtful versus you not regulating your autopilot behavior.
- Consider what would happen if you allowed others to support you without being compelled to return the favor.
- When do you lose focus on how you can best serve the stated purpose of the team/organization by focusing on what you can do to help the individuals on the team or within the organization?
- Write down every time you find yourself changing to fit what others seem to want.

CHAPTER 5

Type 3 Deep Dive

COACH DAVIS WAS IN HIS FIFTH YEAR AS THE VARSITY LACROSSE Coach at Middlebury High School in Massachusetts when a heralded group of freshmen entered the program. The reputation of this group of athletes came with so much fanfare that Coach Davis did not know whether to be excited or cautious, given the expectations and potential egos of the players.

Two weeks into summer conditioning, he realized that he should absolutely be excited. The new athletes were humble, team-oriented, and seemed to have no sense of entitlement. Coach Davis had big plans for what the next four years would look like. He had a particular interest in an athlete named Jeff Speakes. He was the surefire leader of the group of ninth graders and reeked of Division I talent.

The rest of the summer work went as planned, and Coach Davis's enthusiasm grew in the fall and winter months as the team absolutely attacked the weight room. Not only were players showing up, but they were checking up on each other and making sure their teammates showed up too. This is something that Coach Davis had preached since he had been the head coach but had yet to get the athletes to do.

The excitement continued to grow around Middlebury's program and Coach Davis, who traditionally deflected such niceties, leaned into them this time around. He did not downplay the talent of the incoming group, and he openly discussed the potential of the team and aspirations to bring home the school's first lacrosse state championship in the next four years.

Chapter 5

At home, one night Coach Davis was having a heart-to-heart with his wife. She asked if he had any reservations about the group of ninth graders and how they might progress as they grow. He acknowledged that everyone matures at different rates, and other athletes may surpass this group in terms of athletic ability, but he was confident that their skill level and teamwork ethic would persist. He also joked that, while he was not a geneticist, three of the kids had D-1 parents, and he expected them to mature quite nicely. Everything was looking to be pointing in the right direction.

Then, during pre-season practice, the first red flags with this group popped up—particularly with Jeff Speakes. Coach Davis, knowing his team was at least one year from competing for a state championship, decided to schedule the defending champions and top-rated team in the state for a pre-season scrimmage. As expected, Middlebury was getting handled. Down 13–4 late in the game, Middlebury switched to an almost exclusively ninth-grade lineup, and the score immediately bounced to 17–4.

This was the moment when Jeff Speakes asked to be pulled from the game. Coach Davis was in the heat of the game and quickly replaced him. Initially, he thought Jeff was either gassed or dealing with a minor injury of some sort. A few minutes went by and he looked at Jeff to see if he was ready to go back into the game. Speakes just brushed him off. He had decided he was done for the day.

Immediately, a red flag went up for Coach Davis. This was only compounded when he had the team complete their annual goal-setting log. Each season, he asks all his athletes to think of three goals that he, as their coach, can help hold them accountable for working toward. He was taken aback when Speakes handed in his goals with three stated objectives—all about himself. The goals were as follows:

- Make all-tournament team at the Boston Invitational
- Make first team all-newcomer team in conference
- Make at least honorable mention all-conference

While these were all fine goals, Jeff Speakes was the only athlete to not have a single goal about team performance. Moreover, most athletes had a goal of improving their footwork or passing skills or something to that accord for their personal goals. Not Jeff—he was focused on gaining attention and notoriety.

For the first time since this group of ninth graders entered Middlebury, Coach Davis was concerned. Speakes was the unquestioned leader of this group. He was outgoing, gregarious, talented, and ambitious. If Coach Davis did not understand how to productively route Jeff's ambition, this could derail the entire team moving forward.

Coach Davis called Speakes in for a meeting. He did not know exactly how it would go, so he invited his parents to take part in the meeting. Jeff's mom, a coach in a neighboring district, called Coach Davis for some background regarding the reason for calling the meeting. After hearing what the conversation was going to be about, she thought it was best for her son to experience this on his own.

The conversation started with Coach asking Jeff why he did not want to re-enter the blowout loss. Being fourteen, Jeff did not have a well-thought-out and mature answer. But, he was honest. He told the coach that he had never been a part of losing, and definitely never to that extent. He said he did not know how to act, but for the first time in his life, he wanted to be invisible on the lacrosse field. Jeff's honesty paired with Coach Davis's curiosity and desire to help the athlete instead of simply judging him led to a productive conversation about leadership compared to personal image. This resonated with Speakes.

Next, Coach broached the conversation about goals. Jeff was a bit dumbfounded by this question. He asked Coach Davis, in a very respectful manner, what other kids put down because he did not understand how he could be the only one to put all personal accolades down as goals. Coach noted that two other players had one goal that was about personal recognition, but the rest of his entire team was focused on team goals or personal improvement.

Jeff was shocked. His brain had never considered making goals such as that. Coach Davis was extremely happy with how this conversation was going. He had already had a high opinion of the young man, but this conversation was much more open and productive than he had ever hoped for. So, he decided to ask a pointed question to get to the heart of what was driving his future star. He asked Jeff, "Would you rather win 'Massachusetts Player of the Year' or a state championship?" Without hesitation, Jeff answered, "a state championship." This made Coach Davis feel better about the situation, but he also learned that if he was going to work with an athlete as focused on accolades and accomplishments as Jeff was, then he would need to be a constant presence in Jeff's ear reminding him to create team-oriented goals to focus on team-first accomplishments.

With that conversation in the rearview mirror, Coach Davis and Jeff Speakes went on to an incredibly productive and fulfilling relationship. In this scenario, while Coach Davis was not an Enneagram expert, or even an Enneagram novice, he was curious. He took time to get to know his players and to think about them, not only on a behavioral level but also on a motivational level. He understood that, while behavior never lies, understanding the motivation behind the behavior is what provides the leverage to be the best possible coach.

Description of Enneagram Type 3

An Enneagram Type 3 is often called the Achiever. Achievers believe they must perform in order to be successful and to be loved. Love, respect, and adoration are a byproduct of accomplishments and success. As a result, Type 3s have a great deal of personal agency, seem to be constantly in motion and incredibly energetic, are confident, and are goal-oriented.

Type 3s are usually popular and well regarded in the vein of being class president or voted "Most Likely to Succeed." At their best, Type 3s are amazing role models and the true image of success. At their worst, Type 3s can be inattentive to feelings, both their own and others, impatient, and obsessively image-driven. Their behaviors can become focused on wanting to impress others, not just with their talent but also with their superiority. This can manifest or be perceived as narcissistic and nauseatingly self-promotional.

Type 3 Deep Dive

Triad

At first, Type 3s seem not to fit in as part of the Feeling Triad. This is simply because most people would not describe a prototypical Type 3 as someone operating from their feelings. In fact, many Type 3s tend to ignore or compartmentalize their feelings because they feel their feelings may be an impediment to their achievement.

The primary feeling that dominates the subconscious and psyche of a Type 3 is shame. To overcome this core self-image, Type 3s must prove their worth to not only the world but also to themselves. This spurs their insatiable desire for success and recognition as the anecdote to their feeling of shame.

Comparison to Other Types in the Feeling/Heart Triad

Feelings for this triad can be compared to a magnifying glass. Type 2s only want to turn the magnifying glass around to focus on everyone else's feelings, and Type 4s want to use the magnifying glass to look at what's inside of them, to investigate what is missing, in hopes that they can help reclaim the moment. Type 3s want to turn the magnifying glass onto themselves, so everyone else can get a close-up view of them as they garner all the attention.

Motivations

Enneagram Type 3s are motivated by the need to feel valuable and that their life is worthwhile. Type 3s operate from the paradigm that love and acceptance, both internal and external, are derivatives of their performance and success. As such, Type 3s are incredible producers and, when they are engaged in the right types of activity, can create incredible outcomes for themselves and the organizations of which they are a part.

Type 3s have prodigious energy but also tend to run themselves to the point of exhaustion. A Type 3 does not typically quit when the job is done because that means another job needs to be started. A Type 3 finally stops when they have pushed their bodies to the point of breaking, sickness, or exhaustion.

Fear

The basic fear of the Type 3 is of not adding value to a situation, or, worse, being worthless. This fear brings about their seemingly insatiable desire for achievement and to be in the spotlight. The basic actions of a Type 3 operating by default can be characterized by the belief that if you are the highest achieving and most accomplished person around, then people will have no choice but to shower you with love and adoration. Thus, their fear is that if they do not accomplish enough or have sustained success, that they will not be worthy and valuable, adding to their already powerful subconscious feeling of shame.

Craving

Type 3s want unconditional acceptance and adoration. This thirst for prestige and admiration manifests itself in daily behaviors that place achievement and status at a much higher value than all other Enneagram types. When Type 3s are in a healthy emotional place and they are not blindly following this craving, they are incredible leaders and producers. When in peak form, they use their drive for achievement to serve as a beacon of hope for others.

Type 3s, at their best, let their light shine and empower others by doing so. When this craving gets out of control, however, Type 3s can burn themselves out and trample over the needs and feelings of others in pursuit of whatever lofty goal they had previously set for themselves.

Self-Sabotage

The motivation, fear, and craving of the Enneagram Type 3 manifests in self-sabotaging behavior when they are operating on autopilot and do not recognize that they are so focused on achievement that they are taking no joy in the journey. This constant internal pressure to perform leads to self-promotional and egotistical behavior that can lead to them dominating situations and relationships. In many cases, the desire to be recognized for their work in order to feel validated and worthy of adulation drives away people who already care about and love them for who they are.

Additionally, when Type 3s diagnose that the team they are a part of is destined to underperform or fail, a Type 3, who is typically a leader and vocal, will remove themselves from the situation the best they can and slink to the back to avoid being recognized as a member of a failing team or project.

Role on a Team

Type 3s tend to ascend toward leadership or highly visible roles on most teams. As leaders, Type 3s have the ability to produce incredible amounts of work and, frequently, highly successful outcomes. Most Type 3s are outgoing, outspoken, and confident. Their natural ability and willingness to both communicate and to drive hard toward goals lead to many Type 3s being dubbed "natural leaders."

The issue is that the motivation behind these actions can detract from their leadership ability. Additionally, Type 3s can struggle as teammates if the desire for the spotlight and adulation supersedes a Type 3's desire to be a good teammate or to participate on a winning team in which they are not the focus of attention.

Continuum of Behaviors

Every Enneagram type has default behaviors but also a predisposition to behave in different ways depending upon their emotional and behavioral health. When healthy, Type 3s behave like Enneagram Type 6s; and, when under stress, they typically behave like Enneagram Type 9s.

Healthy

Type 3s, who can be boastful and vain, become more cooperative and committed to others, like a Type 6.

Stress

Type 3s, who are outgoing and confident, become withdrawn and consumed by doubt, like a Type 9.

CHAPTER 5

THE ENNEAGRAM

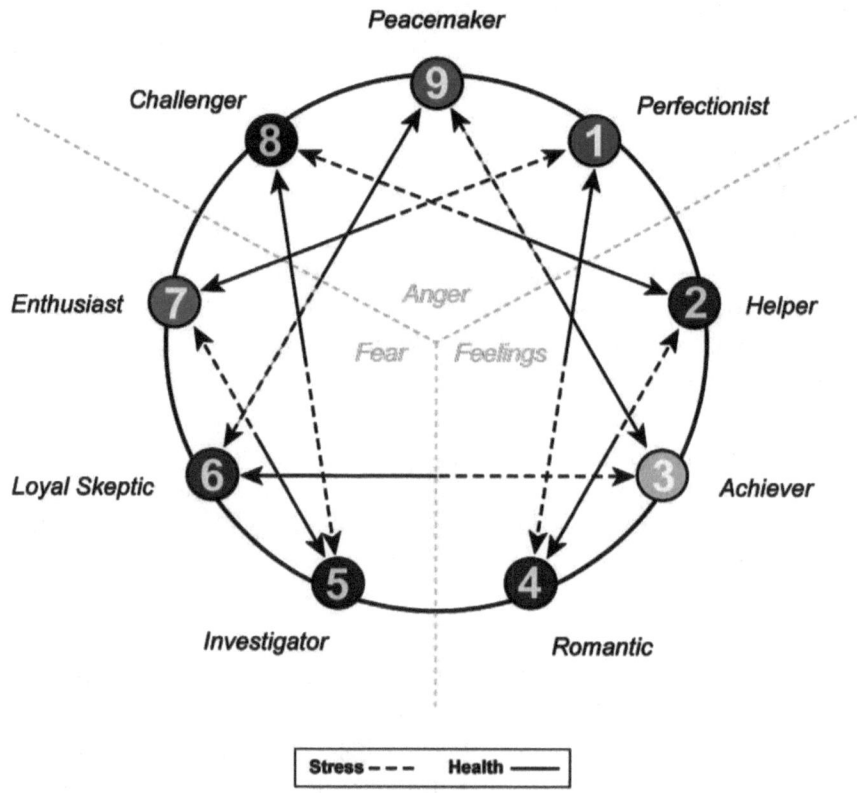

Same, But Different—Enneagram Wings

Although there are nine basic personality types in the Enneagram, each type can be influenced by the types on either side, making two people of the same Enneagram type appear very different. In the case of Type 3s, they can either lean toward Type 2 or Type 4.

Type 3s with a 2-wing tend to be very ambitious, charming, and charismatic. They are very adept at adjusting to their situation and do their best to stand out no matter what crowd they are a part of at the time. They are incredibly gifted at connecting with others and are more concerned with their social standing than other Type 3s. To be clear, all Type 3s are motivated by achievement and success, but Type 3s with a

2-wing are very concerned with their social status and being a part of the in-crowd.

Type 3s with a 4-wing tend to be much more reserved, serious, and introverted than other Type 3s. They still want attention, praise, and success, but tend to be much more serious and reserved than other Type 3s and have earned the moniker "the expert" in many circles.

I might be an Enneagram Type 3 if . . .

- I identify my own worth with accomplishment and success.
- If when my team struggles, I slink to the back when I am normally positioned up front.
- I find joy only in the destination and not in the journey.
- I have worked myself to the point of literal exhaustion or illness.
- I need affirmation from my boss or partner, and if I do not receive it, I will continue to do more work until I am recognized.
- I do not only want to have success at work or at home, I also want to display a wide range of talents.
- There are two outcomes to a competition—winning and losing. Trying hard or performing well but not winning *does not matter*.
- I will do what it takes to blend into my social surroundings, including, but not limited to, always being the politest and most appropriately dressed person in my environment.
- I say things like, "I will sleep when I am dead."
- I tend to crush first impressions.
- I am envious when others, even those closest to me, get praise, and I immediately start plotting how I can earn that praise or level of accomplishment. My image drives my need to work hard and look good.

R^3

Brady Thompson was the kind of kid that every coach dreams of having on his team. He was a three-year starter on one of the best basketball teams in northern Iowa. Brady was voted a team captain as a sophomore, something that had never happened in the twenty-three years that Coach Burton had been the head basketball coach of Lincoln High School. Brady was competitive, tough, possessed a great work ethic, and was a natural leader.

Coming into Brady's senior year, Lincoln High was looking like a good team on paper. They had the potential to make some noise in the state tournament, but no real championship aspirations. Brady was by far the best player, and he made everyone around him better with his energy and drive. That said, they were missing something. They were missing another scorer and someone that could take the load and focus off of Brady. As it stood, if Brady had even a mediocre game, the team would lose.

At the beginning of the summer, the rumor was that Coach Burton's prayers had been answered. A new family had moved into the district from Chicago, and the word was that they had a senior boy who was a great basketball player.

Colin Murry was a 6'4" wing. Coach Burton found limited stats on him from a basketball powerhouse in Chicago. This gave him some pause on the hype train that was already rolling in his small Iowa town. Then came the first practice.

Colin sauntered into that first practice with an incredible air of confidence and every accessory an NBA player could think of. He looked the part. He was sporting an arm sleeve, compression pants under his shorts, wristbands, and new, limited-release Kevin Durant shoes. Everything matched, and everything was in place. This made Coach Burton all the more nervous, since he was not used to having a player that valued their appearance this much.

Then, practice started. It took all of about two seconds of the first summer league practice to see that the rumor of a stud moving in from Chicago was correct. He was quick, explosive, yet silky smooth, all at the same time. The seemingly limitless accessories looked even better when he started playing. Coach Burton was immediately all-in on Colin. The next test would be how he would mesh with Brady.

Colin and Brady hit it off immediately. In fact, Colin gelled with everyone quickly. It was almost as if he had grown up with this group of small-town kids. The team dominated the competition during summer league, and the excitement for what could happen during the season was palpable in the town. The whispers of having two potential all-staters gave hope to the dream of having a state championship team.

The start of the season kicked off as everyone thought. Lincoln High ran through the non-conference portion of its schedule without much of a challenge. Colin got much of the attention with his scoring and his fast-break dunks. Brady did a lot of the dirty work on defense and ran the offense but did not mind the attention going to his teammate. He had the attention for a few years, now he wanted a deep playoff run.

Despite the early season fanfare, everyone knew the season really started during conference play. Three of the past four state champions had come from the conference and this year it was just as loaded. Before Colin arrived, Lincoln was predicted to finish fifth of nine teams in the conference. Dead average.

The first conference game came against nearby Jefferson High, who was the favorite to win the tough conference and ranked third in the state. The crowd was amazing and unlike anything that had taken place at Lincoln in years.

This game, however, was dramatically different from how the season had started. Jefferson had their own 6'5" star player, and he had his way with Colin in the first half. He locked down Colin on defense and seemed to score at will on offense. The player from Jefferson also liked to chirp, and with each hand clap and stare down, Colin would slink further into his own body and out of the play. Colin was in his own head, and Jefferson was in there, as well.

Down by fifteen at the half, Coach Burton tried to rally his troops. Everyone seemed to be reenergized by his rousing halftime speech. Everyone that is, except Colin. He kept his distance from the team, preferring to sit quietly while the others yelled and fired themselves up. Coach Burton noticed this but thought that Colin was just amping himself up after his poor first half. After all, the team had been working together for five months and he had never known Colin to not be an integral part of the team, if not a leader in many instances.

Unfortunately, the second half continued where the first half left off. Lincoln High was no match for Jefferson. Colin, who normally flew up and down the floor, looked defeated. He had no energy and was just jogging around, fully disengaged from his teammates. Brady, however, was playing like his life depended on it. As he willed his teammates to keep fighting and playing hard, they responded. Everyone that is, except Colin; he had checked out.

At one point, after a Jefferson steal, Colin had the opportunity to chase down the player from behind and contest the layup. Instead of giving chase, he just put his head down, walked down the court, tugged on his jersey, signaled for a sub, and asked to be taken out of the game.

Needless to say, this didn't sit well with Brady. He was a captain, and this is not how Lincoln basketball was played. The game ended with Brady and his teammates fighting to keep it close but could never get it closer than twenty. After shaking hands with Jefferson, Brady made a beeline straight to the locker room and to Colin, demanding to know why he had given up on his team. Colin responded with, "What's your problem?"

This touched off a shoving match, and the two had to be separated. Coach Burton sat them both down and told them to squash it. After all, it was only one bad game, and they still had a lot of season to go. Brady, in an uncharacteristic challenge to Coach Burton, asked him why he was letting this slide. All three relationships were impacted. The relationship between the players, as well as between each player and Coach, were forever negatively impacted after that night.

For a season that started with so much promise, it quickly turned into a Jekyll and Hyde exercise. Lincoln looked phenomenal against teams that they should beat but struggled with anyone that could keep up and play with them. Colin would score twenty-five points in one game, then completely disappear during the next when his team needed him the most. Brady continued to grow discontented with this behavior, and Coach Burton was slow to challenge his star transfer.

After one particularly ugly loss during the dog days of the exceptionally long basketball season, the situation came to a head. Not only was Brady angry, but the rest of the team was, as well. It became clear to everyone that Colin was quick to accept the praise when he played well, but wanted no part of digging down, scratching, and clawing when the team was down and needed their most talented player. Led by Brady, the players held a players-only meeting on Sunday after their sixth loss of the season to confront Colin about not giving full effort all the time.

Colin was less than receptive and then told Coach Burton he quit. The season ended exactly how it began—without Colin. Lincoln finished fifth in the conference and had a less-than-strong showing in the postseason. Moreover, Coach lost some credibility in the locker room with the younger guys, and Brady's senior season was a stressful disaster, instead of something he would be able to fondly remember for the rest of his life.

Review

If Coach Burton had an understanding of the Enneagram, he would have surmised that Colin was a Type 3. Colin immediately fit into a new group of kids and quickly ascended to a leadership role alongside Brady. His behaviors clearly indicated this as Type 3s are the most image-driven of all the Enneagram types, almost always extroverted, and desire to project success at all times.

Type 3s will usually be found wearing the latest fashion or "cool" trend to project this image and enjoy the limelight. They are not ones to shy away from cameras. Type 3s also want to avoid any situation where they may fail or where they will be perceived as failing. Thus, Colin's behavior—willfully pulling himself out of a blowout and disappearing when the team was down—fits the Enneagram typing exactly.

Reset

In this scenario, instead of just telling Brady and Colin to "squash" it and minimizing the situation, Coach Burton should have pulled Colin aside and made him aware of his autopilot behavior of hiding from a potential failure. Many Type 3s have no idea that this is their default behavior, and almost no *teenage* Type 3s will come to this realization.

An even more powerful moment could have taken place had Coach Burton exposed the players to the Enneagram at the beginning of the season and made each of them aware of their self-sabotaging behaviors. He then could have shown how both of them were operating on autopilot. Colin with his avoidance, and Brady (Type 8) with his desire to control and willingness to angrily confront his teammate's behavior.

Resolve

The resolution in this scenario would be for Coach Burton to get Colin to focus on team goals, along with his own. Type 3s are primarily driven by individual accolades but can be rechanneled into focusing on team goals that are aligned with personal aspirations. For example, a simple shift from being an all-conference player to playing on a conference champion team might do the trick. In this scenario, Coach could also have set private and personal goals with Colin referencing maximum effort even when the team is struggling. Type 3s thrive on affirmation and frequently do not bother to be concerned with where it comes from or how the affirmation is delivered to them.

Type 3s, when channeled through the lens of the team, are incredible leaders. Their charisma, energy, and competitiveness naturally vault them to these leadership roles. When coaching Type 3s, it is imperative that they are made aware of their self-sabotaging behavior of avoiding any connection with failure.

At best, this manifests as slinking away and blending into the background when things start to sink, but, at worst, Type 3s will quit and walk away before failure can be attributed to them. Focusing them on short-term team goals will keep them engaged because each little victory distracts them from the possibility that they may lose or fail. Also, due to their competitiveness, Type 3s will usually respond very well when they are challenged with a task they have confidence in.

Tomorrow Takeaways

- Take inventory of which ways you are acting as a social chameleon and adjusting to others in search of acceptance and recognition.
- Analyze the last six months of your life and how you have avoided challenges that may have led to failure, and identify when you pushed through the urge to only chase after things you knew you could accomplish.
- Answer the question: What would your life be like if you focused less on doing and more on simply being?
- Identify how you behave and what your reaction is when your emotions bubble to the surface.

Chapter 6

Type 4 Deep Dive

Type 4s will often be the least likely Enneagram type to be playing a traditional team sport. More frequently, Type 4s can be found in the Performing Arts, but nonetheless, still operate as part of a team.

Coach Brandon Smith was a decorated baseball coach in Texas with twelve years of experience. Per most locals, with another decade or so of work, he had a chance at the Texas Baseball Coaches Hall of Fame. That plan was derailed when his military wife was transferred to Virginia.

As they were looking at potential landing spots, a place where he could coach baseball was paramount. The good news was that he found an open program just four miles away from his wife's post, but the bad news was that this team had not posted a winning record in two decades. He would be building the program from scratch. While this was daunting, Coach Smith was oddly excited about the challenge.

Coach Smith always found he had a knack for recruiting athletes and was up to the challenge of trying to build a program at a school that could only field a varsity team the year before. When he arrived, he did all the things all coaches do to recruit. He held open gyms, talked with other coaches to see what athletes did not have a sport in the same season baseball was played, and made himself visible at anything baseball-related in the general vicinity of the school. However, Coach Smith had a secret weapon that most other coaches didn't.

He was a drama teacher and had always found a knack for getting some kids out for athletics that had previously only been involved in the performing arts. Once school started, he was consistent (perhaps relentless) in trying to get as many people out for baseball as possible by promising a fun experience without the gatekeeper protocol of tryouts and cuts. To everyone's surprise, on the first day of practice, over thirty athletes showed up for Coach Smith.

After the first few practices, he found some "diamonds in the rough," and, of course, others who appeared to have never picked up a baseball before. He was happy for both. After all, this was the start of something new, and there was no pressure to win at this point. All he had to do was help these kids grow and start to build a program.

After two weeks of practice, he realized that one of the kids who clearly had never picked up a baseball before just might be one of those "diamonds in the rough" mentioned before. Cole Reynolds was a 6'3" sophomore, who looked more like the bass player in your local band than an athlete, but, man, was this kid a natural athlete. After just two weeks, he was above average, albeit for this group of players, at every baseball skill. He was a decent hitter, fielder, and thrower, and he could not only put the ball in play but also hit for power.

Before the first game, Coach Smith committed to giving each player a performance analysis and a projection, both for this season and their remaining time in the program. Coach was darn near giddy for his conversation with Cole because of how much growth he had exhibited in the few short weeks of practice before the conversation.

He was very surprised by the direction of the conversation. Coach shared with Cole that not only could he start in left field this year but also in the future he could potentially pitch and play the field and perhaps grow into an all-conference player. Cole responded with how he felt about all of the different elements of practice in a very thoughtful but emotional dialogue. He then shared with Coach that he only wanted to do one thing.

Cole had decided that he wanted to be a relief pitcher. He shared that when Coach showed the team videos of games—in an effort to try to build a love of the game within the players—and he saw a reliever walk in with entrance music and many with hair that looked like his, he knew that was what he was destined to do. Coach Smith explained that most high schools do not have a "closer," per se and that most players also played the field.

Cole listened and understood. However, he was adamant; he was going to be a relief pitcher. He assured Coach Smith that he was committed to becoming the best he possibly could at perfecting this skill. Coach Smith did not know how to respond to this. Part of him loved the honesty and self-awareness that this fifteen-year-old kid just exhibited; the other part of him wanted to make this kid understand what it meant to be part of a successful team.

After thinking about the conversation for two days and how he should handle young Mr. Reynolds, he called in the ace he had up his sleeve. His wife was a psychologist for the government, and her job was to understand people, and, in many cases, to understand them better than they understood themselves. He typically tried to avoid using her as a resource because he never felt he could accurately give her a full picture of who the young person he was coaching truly was. This case, however, had him stumped, and he needed help.

After explaining the situation to his wife, who also did not typically love being thrust into these conversations, she gave him advice that would prove to be absolutely spot on. And, she seemed to like delving into this particular situation with him.

She likened Cole to a performer. She explained that while Brandon looked at pitching as a skill, Cole would see it as an art form. The proposition of becoming better in *all* of baseball would simply detract from his becoming an expert in the specialization that he was passionate about. In fact, trying to force him to assimilate into the team would be a negative experience for all involved. She advised that if he let Cole explore becoming the best relief pitcher he could, he would connect with the team in a unique way and assured him that he would not behave like a prima donna or elitist.

His wife's advice was, indeed, flawless. Coach Smith, for the first time in his career, allowed an underclassman to enter into a very specialized role when his talent may have benefited the team in other ways. As a result, Cole's work ethic in thinking about his role on the team as an art form became contagious, and Cole's unique personality served to galvanize the team. He became known as the "vibe keeper" on the team and kept things appropriately loose at all times in the dugout and locker room.

Thanks to the advice of his wife, Coach Smith did not try to force Cole into a more traditional role. Her expertise allowed her to quickly understand that Cole was not a traditional athlete and that differentiating his experience would lead to success. She was exactly right and helped to save Coach Smith from making a significant mistake. Enneagram would have led him to the same conclusion after realizing Cole Reynolds was a typical Enneagram Type 4.

Description of Enneagram Type 4

An Enneagram Type 4 is often referred to as "the Romantic." Type 4s are creative, introspective, empathetic, and reserved. They have a fundamental belief that something is inherently missing, and, without it, they will never be complete. They are in constant search for love or a situation that is unique, special, and fulfills whatever it is that they are drawn to look for, but cannot actually articulate what they are seeking.

As a result, they focus most of their attention and energy inward on their own feelings and emotions. It is this single-minded focus that leads to Type 4s not just feeling their emotions and feelings, but actually living them . . . intensely.

This intensity leads Type 4s down one of two paths. When they are self-aware and moving in a healthy direction, this emotional intensity leads to an incredible amount of creativity and authenticity. However, when Type 4s are on autopilot and their focus drifts to what is missing from their lives, this emotional intensity leads to them withdrawing, being self-absorbed, and being overly sensitive.

Triad

As part of the Feeling Triad, 4s internalize their feelings and are constantly examining them, looking for what makes them different from everyone else. Type 4s demonstrate the need to be a unique individual. Type 4s' core feeling of shame often manifests in an attempt to project an image of being different and out of the ordinary. This can lead to Type

4s appearing as caricatures of the stereotypical eccentric performer or of a whimsical poet that may appear in a Hallmark movie.

A Type 4's deep introspection is aimed primarily at answering the question, "Who am I?" Their core driver of shame leads many Type 4s to the perpetual struggle to figure out their place in the world, their purpose in life, and what essential piece of their life they are missing. These existential questions can lead Type 4s into a constant state of dissatisfaction, always desiring that which is not attainable and wanting something that is forever out of reach. Conversely, when Type 4s believe they have found the answer, they can be very outspoken and proud of their individualism and what sets them apart. This sense of "genius" often leads to further isolation, and the typical melancholy, or even depression, that Type 4s often fight against.

Comparison to Other Types in the Feeling/Heart Triad

Feelings for this triad can be compared to a magnifying glass. Type 2s only want to turn the magnifying glass around to focus on everyone else's feelings, and Type 3s want to turn the magnifying glass onto themselves so everyone else can get a close-up view of them as they garner all the attention. Type 4s want to use the magnifying glass to look at what's inside of them and to investigate what is missing, in hopes they can help reclaim the moment.

Motivations

Enneagram Type 4s are motivated by the need to find themselves and their significance in life. In their eternal quest to "find themselves," they typically discover unique gifts and talents that others do not possess. However, because of their belief that they are missing something, Type 4s frequently have a low sense of self-esteem and a negative self-image.

These tendencies push them to focus on that which makes them different from everyone else. This focus enables Type 4s to be incredibly creative with both the image they portray to the world and in sharing their unique talents with others. The downside of this focus is that it results in them wallowing in self-pity and withdrawing from the people and groups they want to connect with.

Fear

The basic fear of Type 4 is of being ordinary and having no identity or significance. Left unchecked, this fear manifests itself in an overdeveloped flair for the dramatic and expressiveness. As a result, many Type 4s build their identities in an effort to be different from the norm and others. Thus, when unchecked, a Type 4 will push everything to the extreme. This is great for creative works of genius but can serve to isolate them from others with overly expressive and distracting responses to social encounters, expressions of emotions, or eccentric aesthetics, venturing as far away from the status quo as possible.

Craving

Type 4s want to find what is missing. In an effort to find this and express their authentic self to others, Type 4s have vivid and rich imaginations, and a unique ability to communicate their perceived version of reality. These tools allow Type 4s to express incredible creativity and to share their work with the world proudly.

Some of the most beautiful artwork, music, and poetry in the world was produced by Type 4s. However, creativity is not limited to the arts, as one may surmise. Some of the most elegant computer programs and codes have been created by Type 4s, as well as some philosophical paradigms used in all walks of life. These unique works are a Type 4's attempt to contribute to the world, and to help identify what is missing in both their lives and in the world.

Self-Sabotage

The motivation, fear, and craving of the Enneagram Type 4 manifests in self-sabotaging behaviors when a Type 4 is operating on autopilot and does not realize that they are sinking further and further into withdrawal and depression due to focusing on their perceived inability to fit in, and their inability to identify and find what is missing in their lives.

Type 4s self-sabotage when their focus on what they don't have blinds them from what they have to offer the world with their tremendous creativity. So, instead of expressing their creative potential in productive ways, they choose eccentric and erratic behavior to further separate themselves. By operating from their default and resorting to unique expressiveness, they often further isolate themselves and damage their already low self-esteem. This can lead to more acts of expressiveness, which can exacerbate the behavior and lead to a cycle of self-sabotage.

Role on a Team
Type 4s will typically stay on the fringes of a team. Their withdrawn nature and disdain for conformity tend to push them away from leadership roles. However, Type 4s who are allowed to be creative can be invaluable in keeping a team loose before big games and offer comic relief during the dog days of practice. As coaches, Type 4s can make excellent assistants bringing creativity to schemes, play calling, and keeping everyone on their toes. The tendency that must be watched is them (players and coaches) becoming emotionally overwhelmed and sinking deeply into melancholy, sometimes borderline depression, when performance suffers or ideas go unrecognized for the potential genius the Type 4 might feel they possess. In such situations, they can become a negative cancer to a team because they will seek out others that are struggling, dragging them further into the abyss.

Continuum of Behaviors
Every Enneagram type has default behaviors, but also a predisposition to behave in different ways depending upon their emotional and behavioral health. When healthy, Type 4s behave like Enneagram Type 1s; and when under stress, they typically behave like Enneagram Type 2s.

Healthy
Type 4s, who can be dramatic and envious, become more objective and idealistic, like a Type 1.

Stress
Type 4s, who are usually empathetic, yet aloof, take on the worst qualities of a Type 2 and become needy and manipulative.

CHAPTER 6

THE ENNEAGRAM

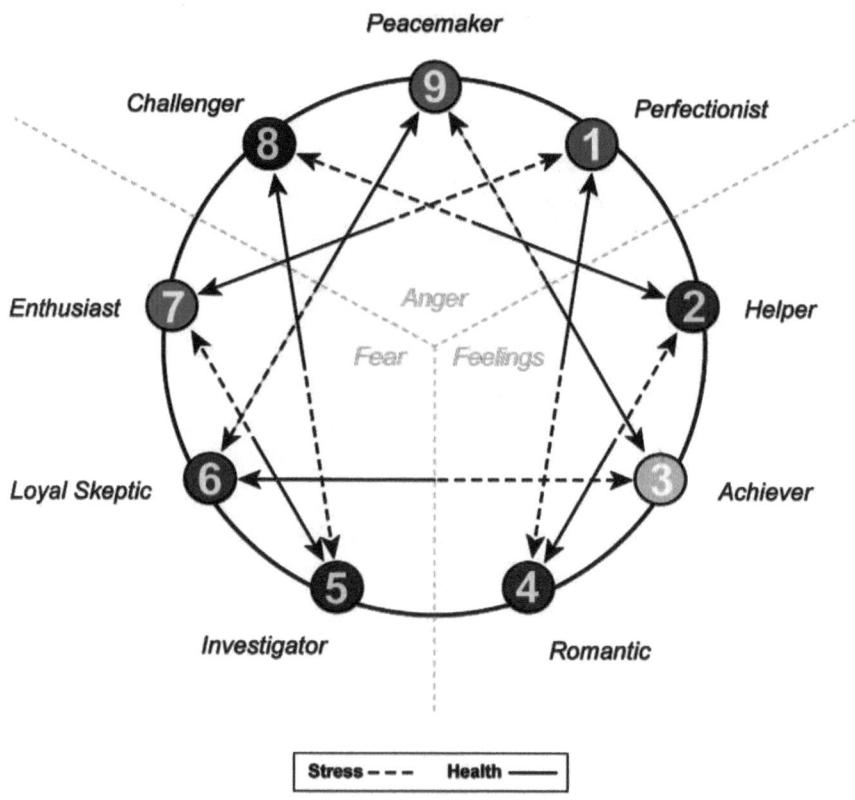

Same, But Different—Enneagram Wings

Although there are nine basic personality types in the Enneagram, each type can be influenced by the types on either side, making two people of the same Enneagram type appear very different. In the case of Type 4s, they can either lean toward Type 3 or Type 5.

Type 4s with a 3-wing want to be not only unique but also the best. They are energized by competition and a desire to win. They tend to be more outgoing, which for a Type 4 often means being even more over-the-top and dramatic. They are also very productive, turning all their thought and imagination into action, and bringing their dreams into reality. Both of these qualities feed into the Type 4 wing-3's desire to stand out and be different.

Type 4s with a 5-wing tend to be much more introverted and eccentric. They still want to differentiate themselves but have less of a need to be noticed by the crowd. They have a much tighter grip on their emotions and feel less compelled to share their feelings or act out. Type 4s with 5-wings are often introverted, not seeking what is missing from their life externally, but often searching for that satisfaction internally. This Type 4 is much less productive and prone to overthinking instead of action.

I might be an Enneagram Type 4 if...

- I am overly dramatic in my reactions to my feelings and everyday situations.
- I have never really felt like I belonged, and this manifests into a feeling I will never find true fulfillment.
- I am self-conscious and find it hard to engage socially with a room full of people unless the engagement revolves around my genius or what makes me unique.
- I often find I am misunderstood by people, which frustrates me.
- I enjoy sad music, movies, and books.
- Overly positive people exhaust me.
- When I need to re-energize myself, I retreat somewhere to be alone.
- I am drawn to the dramatic, unconventional, and macabre. The ordinary bores me.
- I put a great deal of time and thought into my "look," making sure it is original.
- I am envious of many things I do not have, regardless of whether I truly want them or not.
- I will choose my authenticity over almost anything else in the world, even if it leads to suffering. Moreover, I may subconsciously enjoy the suffering.

- When I am told to do something, my first instinct is to do the opposite.
- I am creative and have a ton of ideas, but have little energy or drive to make them reality.

R^3

Central High, a school in a sleepy town in southern Indiana, was a basketball powerhouse. Over the course of a thirty-year career, Coach Thompson had amassed five state championships, ten trips to the Sweet Sixteen, and twenty-three regional championships. With nothing left to prove, and his grandchildren calling, he decided to step down and pass the torch to his longtime assistant, Coach Martin.

Years before, Coach Martin had played on one of Coach Thompson's state championship teams, then continued his career at a small D3 school in Indiana, where he was a Third-Team All-American. Once his playing days were over, he wanted to stay in the game that he loved, so he called Coach Thompson and asked if he had any place on his staff for him. Knowing the type of player he was, Coach Thompson jumped at the chance to mentor his former player.

Coach Martin was a sponge and soaked up all the knowledge that Coach Thompson offered. He felt that what made Coach Thompson so effective was his ability to get all of his players to play as a team, not as a bunch of individuals. He had rules for *everything*. He was a true disciple of the Wooden Rules for Success.

That meant that everyone dressed the same. At the first practice of the season, Coach Thompson would painstakingly take the time to go over all of his rules for success. Everyone was to wear the same shoes, socks, and warm-ups. He made everyone wear the same Central High player "uniform" to school on game days. He even had a rule as to how long his players' hair could be.

Now, Coach Martin didn't like the rules when he was a player, but after a few years of coaching, he began to understand the effect they had on bringing the team together. So, when it was time for him to take over, he kept all of Coach Thompson's rules and traditions intact. He had a talented team coming back and wanted to keep the status quo.

At the first practice, Coach Martin sat down with his team and, almost verbatim, went through Coach Thompson's rules for success. During his talk, he couldn't help but notice a new face whose mind seemed to be elsewhere. Not really being disrespectful, but off by himself, definitely not engaged in learning the "rules." His name was Curtis Barton.

He was a new student at Central that year. His family moved in from Indianapolis right after the start of the school year, and no one really knew much about him since he kept to himself most of the time. The only background that anyone had was that he was a military kid and had been forced to change schools a number of times. Before tryouts, no one even knew he played basketball.

After the first practice, Coach Martin pulled Curtis aside, introduced himself, and asked Curtis if he had any questions about the rules. Curtis was polite and said he did not. Coach Martin replied, "Well, your hair is about as long as it can be. So I would plan on getting it trimmed before our first game." He then asked if Curtis had ever played basketball before, to which he was given the one-word answer of "yes." After an awkward pause waiting for some elaboration, Coach Martin said he was glad to have him on the team and that practice starts at 3:30 p.m. sharp tomorrow after school. This was followed by Coach Thompson's favorite line, "If you're not early, you're late!"

The next day, everything Curtis did stood out. Some in a good way, some not. At 3:30, just as practice was starting, Curtis burst through the doors and joined in the warm-ups for practice. Technically not late but definitely not early. He had two different pairs of socks on, bright pink shorts, and a shirt from his old school. And then, Curtis put on a display of athleticism that Coach Martin hadn't seen since his college days.

With his long, 6'3" frame, he was all over the court. His on-the-ball defense was incredible, frustrating the best ball handlers on the team. He could jump out of the gym and just seemed to know where the ball was coming off the iron every time, collecting rebounds at will.

By the time practice was over, Coach Martin knew he had something special in Curtis but also that he needed to get him on board with conforming to all the team rules. So, he pulled Curtis aside and reminded

CHAPTER 6

him of proper practice attire and that he was expected to be at practice *before* 3:30, not *at* 3:30.

The next day, Curtis showed up at 3:29, wearing the proper color socks, shorts, and shirt. However, this time he was wearing a bright orange headband and had his socks pulled up to his knees. Technically, these weren't against the "rules" but definitely skirted the line. Coach Martin, trying to keep everyone to the rules, pulled Curtis aside after practice and reminded him of what was proper practice attire.

It went like this for the first few weeks of practice. Curtis continued to dominate in practice and scrimmages on the defensive end and rebounding. He also had an innate sense of the offensive and defensive sets Coach Martin was teaching. He never scored much, but he loved to do the dirty work and make all the hustle plays.

Curtis was a paradox. He did all the little things well. He did not demand the ball. He did not seem to care if he fit in. On the court, the only thing he did that made Coach Martin nervous was show too much emotion at times. He never did so in a way to embarrass other people or show anyone up, but he would definitely exhibit some "look at me" behaviors. However, he did so in a nontraditional sense. It was more often his desire to dive across the floor or smack the ground when intense on defense, but it still was not the norm for the program. On one hand, he was a coach's dream; on the other hand, he made Coach Martin very uncomfortable with his clear desire to not conform to the team rules.

Unfortunately, Curtis couldn't seem to grasp the concept of all of Coach Martin's rules. Coach Martin pondered this often and tried to discern whether he could not grasp the concepts, or simply refused to grasp the concepts. It became exhausting, and it seemed that every practice ended with another conversation about what Curtis couldn't wear. Because of his repeated stretching of the team rules, Coach Martin said he couldn't start the opening game.

Curtis was not happy, but, as was usual with him, he didn't say much.

On the day of the first game, Curtis showed up to school wearing the proper "uniform" to school, and everyone thought that maybe Curtis had run out of ways to stand out as an individual, finally embracing this role on the team. That thought remained until game time. As per usual,

Curtis showed up about one minute before everyone was required to be there. He walked into the locker room with his hood up, wearing everything he was supposed to, and sat quietly in the corner until it was time to take the court.

He pulled his hood down and everyone's, including Coach Martin's, jaw hit the floor. Curtis had dyed his hair purple. Not just purple, but bright purple. Coach Martin walked right up to Curtis and told him there was no way he was playing with that hair.

Curtis snapped. He said, "You make up all of these stupid rules, and I am following all of them now. You never said anything about the color of our hair. Length yes, but not the color. So what rule am I breaking now?" Coach Martin didn't have an answer. It was his first game as a head coach, and Coach Thompson never had to deal with something like this. So, he told Curtis to sit on the bench for the entirety of the game and they would talk about it after the game had ended.

The game didn't go well, and Central was drubbed by twenty-five. After the game, Curtis met Coach Martin in his office and told him that he respected his rules, but if he couldn't express himself, he didn't want to play. Coach Martin was stuck. After the public confrontation in front of the team, if he gave in, he would look weak. If he held his position, then he would be cutting off his nose to spite his face. He was stuck!

Review
In this scenario, Coach Thompson and, by extension, Coach Martin were Type 1s that valued rules and order above everything, with no exception. This type of leadership works well for most types. However, Curtis was a Type 4 whose self-expression and desire for authenticity were at the top of his hierarchy of needs. An understanding of the Enneagram types of his players would have brought Coach Martin to this conclusion, well before the public confrontation leading to an abrupt benching at the first game.

Reset
After repeated attempts by Curtis to express his uniqueness, Coach Martin had multiple opportunities to sit down with Curtis and ask him why

he continued to try to break, or at least bend, his rules. However, Coach Martin's own autopilot of resenting anyone who tried to break his rules led him to keep doubling down on them.

Curtis attempted to follow the rules. He was not attempting to rebel. He, however, had an innate desire to be his own unique person. As Curtis continued to find different ways to stand out, the coach had many opportunities to proactively solve this dilemma and to do so collaboratively with Curtis. Without taking that step, Curtis and Coach were on a collision course dictated by the autopilot behaviors dictated by their Enneagram types.

Resolve

The resolution, in this case, would have been for Coach Martin and Curtis to have a conversation about the ways in which Curtis could still live within the rules but be free to differentiate himself from the ordinary. Finding a common ground would have enabled Curtis to not only express himself as a unique individual but also thrive as a member of the team. His desire to be amazing on the court at defense and rebounding, and his lack of desire to be the person showing up on the scoreboard, was driven by the same motivation that led to him dying his hair purple. Coach Martin could have leveraged this to drive toward peak performance, instead of allowing it to lead them into interpersonal conflict.

Type 4s are probably the most image-conscious of all the Enneagram types. Their desire to stand out and avoid looking ordinary takes high precedence in their lives. In many cases, the desire to be unique is valued over what appears to be clearly in their own self-interest.

As a result, Type 4s like Curtis can look rebellious, when in reality, they are just trying to express themselves. When leveraged appropriately, this can lead to bringing a team together in creative ways, as a Type 4 gives implicit permission for everyone to let themselves be their authentic selves. When not thoughtfully approached by the coach, however, this can lead to self-destructive behavior from the Type 4 and perhaps even lead to removal from the team.

As said at the beginning of the chapter, Type 4s are the least likely Enneagram type to be playing team sports. While this is true, one has to wonder how many Type 4s are run off teams because coaches don't have the training to recognize what these types look like and to adjust their style to best reach each athlete.

Too often, coaches can lose the forest through the trees. Instead of seeing a quiet kid with a unique set of skills that can help the team, coaches see a "trouble-maker" or "rebel" that refuses to conform to team rules. The intent of this book, and the training that can be provided to explore the Enneagram, is to open up opportunities for kids that don't fit into the "sports" box.

Tomorrow Takeaways

- Analyze the last six months of your life for how many times you have become overly emotional or gotten swept up in your emotions, and how that behavior has negatively impacted your relationships.
- Write down all of the creative ideas and thoughts you have. Then, make action plans for each one to bring them into reality.
- Chart how much time you spend focusing attention and energy on what is missing from your life.
- Create a gratitude journal to express appreciation for the people and opportunities around you, taking your focus away from what you think is missing.
- Evaluate whether you feel pride in being special and unique, or whether your behaviors are borne out of shame in being less than your ideal self.

Chapter 7

Type 5 Deep Dive

When a new principal was hired at Coal City High School, one of the first major changes publicly announced was that no athletic team would be "cutting" athletes for reasons other than conduct and behavior. Translation—even the least athletic students would have a spot on the team of their choosing.

The new directive came with two caveats that eased many coaches' minds. First, there was zero expectation of playing time for students at the high school level. Essentially, kids could be part of any program they chose but should not expect to play if their talent and skill level were not commensurate with what was necessary to have success. The second caveat was that, in the instance that there were too many additional players within a program, the district would fund additional assistant coaches.

These two caveats made the rule, although still met with resistance, much more bearable for the experienced coaches within the school. Coach Katz was known to be strong and disciplined, and her practices were legendary. Many successful young women in the community credit Coach Katz with instilling discipline in them and giving them the tools to advance themselves to new levels of both concentration and fitness.

Given this reputation and the common sense caveats to this new directive, Coach Katz had nothing to say about it when the coaches would get together for conversation and coffee. Internally, she knew that very few people who were not serious about softball would be interested in giving all she demanded just to be part of the program.

Chapter 7

She was right. In the year following the new school mandate, she only had four "additional" athletes across all levels of the program than she had the year before. Three of the girls were relatively unskilled but actually helped push the team forward because of how badly they wanted to compete.

One athlete, however, did not quite fit. She was not exactly what Coach Katz would call lazy, but she was awfully close. This new addition to the program was more skilled than the other newbies but did not take much initiative and did the absolute bare minimum to meet the physical demands of being part of the team. To be honest, this frustrated Coach Katz to no end and made her question why this athlete, Anna Barr, was out for the team in the first place. After all, practices were very demanding physically; Coach couldn't figure out why Anna was choosing to put herself through the work that she seemed to clearly resist—particularly without any guarantee of playing time.

Then, late in the third week of practice, bad weather made outdoor practice impossible and the gyms were unavailable for use. While these days were an annoyance, Coach Katz secretly loved them, because they gave her the opportunity to show videos and teach the game as though it was a course in school. The girls typically did not love this activity, and, honestly, many clearly wished that they would just receive an unscheduled day off.

That afternoon, she planned to show videos of the gold-medal-winning 2004 US Olympic Softball team. As she began to introduce the history of the team, Anna jumped in and essentially taught the lesson. To Coach Katz's sincere shock, Anna Barr was a true student of the game! To think, Coach had secretly thought Anna to be a bit lazy, but the truth was, she was deeply intellectually interested in the game they both loved.

After the meeting, Coach pulled Anna aside and was honest with her about her shock. Anna went on and on about the beauty of the game and talked through scenarios with Coach that she found particularly interesting. Coach thought they had a breakthrough moment, which they sort of did, but not in the way she originally thought. The next day, they went out to practice and Anna's effort, again, was just enough to get by.

Coach Katz was confused, but the lack of overall energy and outward enthusiasm brought forward by Anna was no longer as annoying to Coach as it was just a few days earlier. In fact, the next several weeks were non-descript for Anna. The season started. She was not playing. She was quiet on the bench and did nothing to stand out positively or negatively. The season was just passing by.

Then, nearly a third of the way through the season, Coal City played Beachwood for the second time. After the second inning, in which Beachwood stole five bases on the way to four runs, Anna, surprisingly, approached Coach Katz. Coach Katz was not in the mood for Anna to want to talk about playing time at this juncture of the season, but Anna surprised Coach Katz yet again.

She leaned over and whispered something in Coach's ear. Coach Katz's face looked to be in thought and somewhat confused. Coach asked a question, and Anna leaned back in, and whatever she said set a light bulb off in Coach's head. The conversation ended with Coach asking Anna if she was sure and Anna confirming.

Between innings, Coach called the team together and announced what she believed was the steal sign for the other team. The team listened, then went out into the field to start the next inning. Like clockwork, the first batter of the inning reached, and then, on the third pitch, the steal sign was given from the Coach to their runner on first. This time though, the entire Coal City defense was ready, and the runner was easily thrown out at second base. The momentum of the game entirely shifted at that moment.

On the ride home, Coach Katz grinned to herself thinking about the complex young woman that Anna was proving to be. Coach thought she was getting just one more athlete in Anna at the beginning of the season, but it turned out she was getting a student of the game, in addition to a de facto assistant coach.

Once Coach Katz realized what she had in Anna, she leveraged Anna's talent. She had an observer. She had someone who was intellectually curious about the game of softball. She had an athlete who was thoughtful and comfortable being independent. Given all of these things, it became standard practice for Coach Katz to walk by Anna at least twice a game and ask, "What are you seeing?"

There were times when Anna had nothing for Coach, but there were times when her insights were game-changers for the team. Anna's ability to be thoughtful and critically observe her team, analyzing the game she loved, brought incredible value and joy to Anna, Coach Katz, and, most surprisingly, the program.

Description of Enneagram Type 5

An Enneagram Type 5 is also called "the Investigator." As this name implies, Type 5s are inquisitive and driven to accumulate as much knowledge as possible. They are analytical, detached, and private people who, more than anything, want to understand how the world works.

Type 5s typically won't be found in leadership or social roles. Their preference is to observe and understand, not to participate. Type 5s would likely prefer to be alone studying for the next test, analyzing game film, or breaking down a book on game theory, instead of socializing or team building. This positions them perfectly for the role of an expert in whatever field they are invested in, being able to absorb, deconstruct, and synthesize complex ideas, concepts, and skills.

Their intense focus can lead to remarkable discoveries and innovations. However, Type 5s default to observation is a result of their scarcity mindset when it comes to their own energy. They believe they only have so much energy to give to the world, and they can conserve it by remaining emotionally distant and observing, instead of engaging. Type 5s choose to live more in their minds than to expend energy in activity, leading them to frequently appear emotionally distant or intellectually arrogant.

Triad

As part of the Fear Triad, Type 5s use their fear as motivation, preferring to battle it in the arena of the mind. Their drive is to accumulate as much knowledge, energy, and resources as possible to insulate themselves against their fears of being useless or incapable.

Unfortunately, this drive is a direct result of their insecurity and fear about their ability to successfully navigate through the world. This accumulation of knowledge and understanding makes Type 5s appear confident, self-sufficient, and immune to fear. But when it comes time to act on all the knowledge and resources they have collected, which would boost their confidence, they often retreat into the comfort and safety of their minds.

Type 5s operate their lives from the mindset of the old saying "Better to keep your mouth shut and be thought of as a fool, than to open it and remove all doubt."

Comparison to Other Types in the Fear/Head Triad

Fear in this triad can be compared to a rumor. Type 6s are scared of the rumor but must express this fear and share their feelings with anyone who will listen. Type 7s understand the rumor exists but choose to numb themselves to the rumor and distract themselves with any other activity that can occupy their mind. Type 5s understand that the rumor exists and want to repress it so badly that they may move to another town so as not to have to engage with it.

Motivations

Enneagram Type 5s are motivated by the need to be competent, capable, and to understand the world around them. The more knowledge and resources they can accumulate, the more they are insulated from the demands that life presents. Moreover, as life presents demands, the more understanding they possess, the less likely they are to seem incapable.

This usefulness manifests in several ways. The Type 5's preference to observe from the periphery, rather than to engage in activity, allows them to be objective during decision-making. They have a unique ability to sort through all the facts, look at a situation from every conceivable angle, and come up with an unbiased decision. This skill set positions them well to be the analytical arm of any team or organization.

Unfortunately, this same skill set often prevents Type 5s from engaging in life. It is much safer to sit in contemplation than to put yourself out there for the world to see. Life is better to be understood than to be lived, in the mind of a Type 5.

Fear

The basic fear of a Type 5 is of being, or appearing, foolish, useless, or incapable. This fear is expressed in the reluctance of Type 5s to engage with unique complexities that define human-to-human interaction.

They believe that they only have so much energy to give to the world and that the world's demands are just too great. Thus, Type 5s become very adept at compartmentalizing everything in their lives, and they will only meter out a specific amount of energy to maintain each compartment. Their friends, job, relationships, hobbies, and so on are all assigned to specific mental boxes, and they will often deal with one box at a time. As soon as the reserved mental energy for that compartment is tapped out, Type 5s extricate themselves and move on—frequently, to some much-needed alone time to recharge.

This behavior, borne out of fear, protects Type 5s from spending too much time in any area that may expose them as not having all the answers, which they believe would render them useless.

Craving

Type 5s crave self-sufficiency and autonomy. They never want to be put into a position where they have to rely on others, or even have the perception of reliance on others. As such, Type 5s rarely, if ever, ask questions in a situation where they are not expected to be learners. They prefer to figure it out themselves through observation, study, and intellect.

As a result of this craving and their desire for self-containment, Type 5s are typically minimalists. They view the accumulation of possessions and authority as just more things that they will have to spend time thinking about, maintaining, or replenishing. This line of thinking even shows up in the way they dress. Everything is utilitarian. Image is definitely not on the radar of a Type 5. An image that may help to enforce this message is that of the disheveled professor who wears the same old sweater each day.

Self-Sabotage

The motivation, fear, and craving of the Enneagram Type 5 manifest in self-sabotaging behavior when a Type 5 is operating on autopilot and does not recognize that their focus on knowledge accumulation and conservation of energy leads to isolation and the appearance of intellectual arrogance. Of all the types, Type 5s are the most emotionally detached. After all, feelings and emotions require a lot of energy. This detachment can come off as cold and calculating, hindering relationship development. As a result, Type 5s can struggle not only in leadership roles but also in personal relationships, which only pushes them more and more into isolation.

Another self-sabotaging behavior of Type 5s is that of not engaging in life. Their fear of looking foolish, along with their need to know everything, makes them very risk-averse. Thus, their preference is to observe, as opposed to actually trying something new. Knowledge accumulation is often only theoretical instead of experiential, which ultimately leads them to be less impactful and even less self-sufficient.

Role on a Team

Type 5s will congregate in the back of the pack during a drill watching what is going on unless they are absolutely confident they understand all of the ins and outs of the drill. Type 5s disdain being called on to demonstrate anything new. An activity like walking through new plays is incredibly stressful for them, and they will often slink off to the side in hopes of not being in the first group to do the work.

Healthy Type 5s might ascend to a leadership role, but typically they are best suited to a more peripheral role where their objective knowledge and expertise in a specific niche can be best expressed. Type 5s now have become more pronounced in sports as the analytics movement has begun to drive decision-making at the collegiate and professional levels. Most likely, however, you do not know about them. Type 5s don't crave the spotlight and much prefer to be in a position where they have a well-defined assignment and nothing else is asked of them.

CHAPTER 7

THE ENNEAGRAM

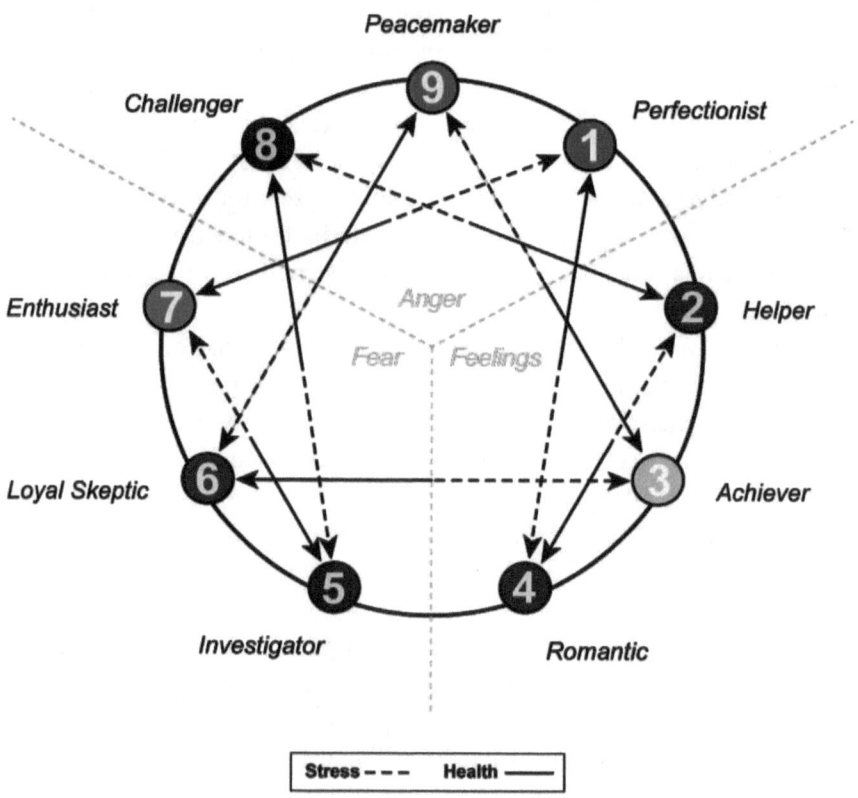

Continuum of Behaviors

Every Enneagram type has default behaviors, but also a predisposition to behave in different ways, depending upon their emotional and behavioral health. When healthy, Type 5s behave like Enneagram Type 8s; and when under stress, they typically behave like Enneagram Type 7s.

Healthy

Type 5s, who can be detached and deliberate, become more self-confident and decisive, like Type 8s.

Stress
Type 5s, who are deliberate and analytical, become scattered and reckless, like Type 7s.

Same, But Different—Enneagram Wings
Although there are nine basic personality types in the Enneagram, each type can be influenced by the types on either side, making two people of the same Enneagram type appear very different. In the case of 5s, they can either lean toward Type 4 or Type 6.

Type 5s with a 4-wing tend to be creative, empathetic, and isolated. They still strive for independence but are moved more by image and thus can fall on the more eccentric side. Their mental energy is focused more on the unusual or counterintuitive, thus fulfilling the Type 4's desire to be different.

Type 5s with a 6-wing still tend to be cautious and skeptical but are more social and outgoing than the average Type 5. They still want to live in their head and figure out the world but are much more open to cultivating relationships and sharing their ideas with others.

I might be an Enneagram Type 5 if . . .
- I have very few outfits and/or multiple "sets" of the same outfit.
- I end most days with the thought that I accomplished a lot, only to realize that I spent a majority of it in my head thinking and got no tangible work done.
- I've gotten into disagreements with others over things I thought I told them, but I only had the conversation in my head.
- I feel like the demands the world places on me are never-ending but struggle to identify what those are.
- I am exhausted by the end of the day because I only have so much energy to give.
- I prefer my private life to stay private. No one should know everything about me.
- I would much rather observe than participate.

- I need alone time to recharge my batteries.
- I hoard things I can control, like my time and space.
- I make lists of pros and cons when making decisions. Then, I make the most logical decision, regardless of how others feel.
- I need time to process an experience or information in order to know how I feel about something.
- I have great ideas, but I keep them to myself because I'm not sure they will be correct or accepted.
- I lose myself for hours on the internet "researching" an obscure topic.

R^3

Coach Mike Lewis was the head wrestling coach for Washington High in South Dakota. His family had deep ties to wrestling in South Dakota, as his father had been a head high school coach, and, Mike, along with each of his three brothers, wrestled at different Division III schools throughout the state. His mom joked that they were "wrestling royalty."

After graduation, he quickly found a job as a math teacher at Washington. With his pedigree and tenacity, it was clear that he would be the varsity coach soon. It only took him four years to earn that title.

Three years into his tenure, Coach Lewis was finding his stride as a coach. The program, while it had been consistent under previous coaches, was never able to break through in the state series. They came close a few times but always came up short. As a result, the program never "exploded," and the lack of numbers made it hard to compete at that level.

This seemed to be slowly changing, as the program grew each year under Coach Lewis, and everyone felt like things were moving in the right direction. Coach Lewis's energy and passion for wrestling attracted some of the better athletes at Washington who chose wrestling over basketball, which was never the case a few years earlier.

Washington was entering a new era in which all fourteen weight classes were filled, and there were even some battles taking place in the wrestling room to figure out who would be representing Washington at meets. This internal competition started to show clear results during

Type 5 Deep Dive

meets and tournaments, and there was a palpable buzz building around the program.

Dustin Shaw was an incoming freshman that year and was penciled in as the starter at 113 pounds. Shaw was a state placer in junior high, and the 113 weight class was the weakest one at Washington. Coach Lewis was confident that he could quickly get Dustin up to speed and ready to compete at a high level, even without significant practice competition.

Dustin was a quiet kid. He drew very little attention to himself and spent the majority of his time hanging toward the back of the room. Whether it was math class or the wrestling room, Dustin was content to keep to himself, absorb whatever information he could, and get his work done.

Dustin and Coach Lewis hit it off immediately, largely as a result of building a good rapport during math class, where Dustin was a true standout. Coach Lewis was impressed with his academic gifts, and, knowing what he did about Dustin's wrestling history, thought he may end up with the total package—a standout student-athlete whom he could coach and mentor for four years.

For the first few weeks of practice, everything seemed to be going well. The team was rounding into shape, the leaders were starting to separate themselves from the pack, and the starting lineup was becoming clear. The hole at 113 that Coach expected Dustin to fill was still keeping him up at night, though.

Dustin did what he was supposed to, but his lack of urgency concerned Coach Lewis. By not doing the extra that all other starters were doing, the confidence Coach Lewis initially had was diminishing. Dustin wasn't slacking off or being defiant, Coach Lewis could just tell that Dustin wasn't putting all of his effort into practice every day. Coach, having been around the scene for a long time, knew this would come back to bite Dustin as a *freshman* varsity wrestler.

After thinking about this for a few weeks, Coach Lewis pulled Dustin aside at the end of practice and asked him how everything was going. Dustin was his usual quiet self and said everything was fine. Coach Lewis wasn't satisfied with that answer, so he pushed him a little bit. He told Dustin that he didn't feel like he was putting as much effort into practice as he could be and wanted to know if that was a fair assessment. To Coach Lewis's surprise, Dustin agreed with him and launched into a ten-minute monologue as to all the reasons why he was holding back. It was thoughtful and everything Coach Lewis wanted to hear.

Unfortunately, nothing really changed with Dustin's practice performance, and the lack of fire he showed in practice made its way into his matches as well. Dustin dropped his first four matches of the season. He was wrestling very tentatively. Coach Lewis could not quite describe it until his assistant remarked that it was like he was out there *wrestling not to lose* as opposed to *wrestling to win*. While that is not a great strategy in any sport, it is particularly limiting in wrestling.

The problem was, every time Coach Lewis reviewed film of his matches with him, Dustin always said the right things, then wanted to talk about different techniques he read about online. The extra study work made Coach Lewis believe that Dustin really was committed to wrestling.

After the first two weeks of mediocre team results, Coach Lewis opened up the wrestling room at 6:00 a.m. for those wrestlers who needed extra help or to cut more weight. The athletes knew that these "optional" practices, while technically not mandated, were something they should be at.

Dustin never made it to any of the early morning sessions. When pressed as to why he wasn't coming in, Dustin always had some kind of story about other commitments. He had a school project, he had homework, or he had to take his brother to school. Some were valid, but some were clearly small things that could have been worked out if he wanted to get in the extra mat time.

As the season wore on, Dustin's behavior was becoming as erratic as his wrestling. Noticing it, Coach Lewis tried to motivate Dustin, but talking to him yielded no results since he would just steer the conversation into the minutia of a specific move or strategy and talk incessantly about it. Coach Lewis was frustrated. Given the nature of wrestling and weight classes, there was little he could do to provide accountability because the equivalent of playing time was just about guaranteed for Dustin.

Finally, at one of the biggest meets of the year, everything came down to Dustin's match. If he won, Washington would win a dual meet they had not won in eight years. If he lost, the team lost. It was one of those meets where the stands were packed, every match went down to the wire, and you couldn't hear yourself think because it was so loud. Everyone was on the edge of their seats for this last match.

Coach Lewis, with his adrenaline pumping, yelled at Dustin to get it going. He implored Dustin, "We need your absolute best right now!" Dustin nodded but maintained his usual flat line.

The match was a perfect microcosm of the season for Dustin and Coach Lewis. With his opponent on the offensive the entire time, Dustin seemingly tried to avoid the action. As the time ticked away, Dustin trailed by a point. It was now or never. Coach Lewis shouted at him to attack. But he didn't. Instead, he was taken down as the buzzer sounded.

The gym went crazy, and Coach Lewis was beside himself. Dustin shook hands and walked off the mat like nothing had happened. No expression of disappointment, anger, or regret. Just placid, like he was walking away from doing something as mundane as walking to class.

Coach Lewis had no clue what to do. There was no one behind Dustin, so he couldn't bench him. He didn't even know if that would do any good anyway. How could someone with so much potential just not care? More importantly, as a coach, he was worried he could not maintain the trust of his team if he continued to put someone on the mat at each meet that was not giving the team everything he had. Coach Lewis felt stuck in a no-win situation.

Review

Coach Lewis's exasperation is typical of anyone coaching a Type 5 like Dustin without a better understanding of his default behaviors. Using the Enneagram, Coach Lewis would understand that Type 5s are emotionally detached observers by trait. Above all else, Type 5s don't want to look foolish, and would much prefer to do everything by themselves with no help.

Thus, they have a hard time performing, especially when there is a chance they may lose or fail since that would expose them as not being self-reliant. In some cases, with individual sports like wrestling, they would rather look competent in a close loss than go aggressively after a victory.

When put in stressful situations, Type 5s will disintegrate into the worst traits of a Type 7. They become obsessed with chasing and doing anything except what is important and right in front of them. In this example, instead of coming in for morning training sessions, Dustin found any possible excuse not to attend practice or additional training because he could have been exposed as incapable or reliant on his coaches for help.

A go-to strategy for Type 5s is to avoid work through dialogue or discussion. This is evidenced by Dustin's never-ending stream-of-consciousness about the minutia of some technique or idea. These conversations serve to distract both parties from what is important.

Reset

Coach Lewis had probably never run into a Type 5 before Dustin. This type can be very difficult to connect with since they play everything so close to the chest. Most Type 5s are introverted and, like Type 9s, are typically of low outward energy.

In fact, they only have so much energy in their tank for specific tasks, and once this energy is done, they are done. So, don't expect Type 5s to put in the extra effort. Seriously. The more demands put on a Type 5 to exert beyond what they believe they are capable of will send them spiraling into avoidance behavior.

If Coach Lewis could have taken a moment to recognize this type of behavior, he could have used different strategies to pull the best out of Dustin. As coaches and leaders, we will be responsible for leading and getting the most out of all types of people. A quick reset would have allowed Coach Lewis to find a different strategy to pull Dustin forward.

Resolve

In this scenario, the resolution for Coach Lewis would have been to use film study and practice time to break down specific moves and situations to boost Dustin's confidence. With the confidence that he could be successful in deploying these techniques, Dustin may have become more aggressive on the mat

The reason is simple, the more knowledge and success Type 5s acquire, the more self-confident and assertive they become. The best practice programs for Type 5s involve a lot of repetitive drills for mastery of both skills and situational awareness.

As said earlier, Type 5s can be frustrating to work with. Their finite energy capacity, emotional detachment, and the never-ending need to verbalize their deep and complex thoughts can be enough to drive even the most Enneagram-centric and self-aware coaches over the edge. However, if focused and engaged, Type 5s can be very valuable members of a team.

When not clouded by self-doubt, they make good sound decisions based on logic and not emotion. They also possess a unique quality to absorb and process a tremendous amount of information. As with most Enneagram types, the things that can make them very successful are very connected to the things that can serve as their downfall.

Tomorrow Takeaways

- Analyze how often you don't speak up when you see others making a mistake or poor decision. How do these times of inaction hurt yourself and your team's success?
- Identify the areas or scenarios that cause you to freeze. What fears are driving this behavior? Is it a fear borne out of the image of looking foolish or not having all the answers? How does this fear inhibit you from making an impact?
- Journal all the ways you feel intruded upon by others, your job, and the world for a week, and identify, objectively, which of those things are truly demanding more of you than you are capable of giving.
- Ask yourself, "What happens to all the energy I don't use on a given day in my attempt to hoard my precious personal resources?"

CHAPTER 7

- Get out of your comfort zone. Pick up a new hobby or habit that you know nothing about, and dive in head first. Make it something physical that you have to perform in front of others.
- Start an exercise program. Get out of your head, and focus on your body and your health.

Chapter 8

Type 6 Deep Dive

Coach Walton was walking to his car after school one day and meandered by the practice fields as he often did. The practice field behind East Devlin High School was where it was likely to find a game of pick-up football going during the off-season. Coach loved to see the kids playing and also got a kick out of how one day he would see high schoolers playing, then the next day a group of third graders playing touch football. He loved the game and loved that his community felt the same way.

One day he was walking by and saw a bunch of his ninth-grade students playing a game of seven-on-seven. He stopped for a minute to watch, and an athlete immediately caught his attention. Two things jumped out. First, his freak athleticism. Second, he had no idea who the kid was. As both a teacher and a coach, this was really rare. He joked to himself that he may have to deal with guarding this exceptional athlete next season.

Coach watched for about ten minutes, then got in his car to head home. The next morning, while Coach Walton was enjoying a coffee and making playful conversation with students in the hallway, the captain of the ninth-grade football team walked by. Coach pulled him quickly into his classroom and asked about the incredible athlete playing on the practice field last night.

The captain told him that it was a new kid named Avery, who had moved in from Wisconsin earlier this year. Coach asked all the typical questions. Is he a good kid? Does he get good grades? The list of questions continued until the captain said something that shocked Coach

Chapter 8

Walton. He shook his head and said, "We've tried, Coach. Avery says he won't play for the team."

At that moment, Coach Walton decided he was on a mission. Avery was going to play football for East Devlin High School, there were no two ways about it. After school, Coach sought out Avery and gave him the typical recruiting talk; Avery politely declined. For the next four months, Coach did this, and every single day, Avery responded in the same way.

Finally, Avery asked why Coach Walton cared so much about whether he played or not.

Coach Walton answered in a reasonable way. He talked about how students involved in athletics performed better academically than their peers. He noted that the leadership skills taught in football would prepare Avery for the real world. He concluded with the fact that there were very few situations in the world where a person becomes as bonded to another group of people as in football.

Avery politely nodded, but this answer just pushed him further away. He knew the real answer to his question was that Coach Walton thought he could help his team win games, and he never mentioned that once. The four months of trust that Coach had worked so diligently to build went by the wayside in that single moment.

The next season rolled around, and Avery was noticeably absent from tryouts, two-a-days, and the preseason. He clearly had stuck to his convictions and was not going to be playing football. Coach Walton, consumed with the season, quit investing so much time in trying to get Avery out to play. As Avery had guessed, and Coach's behavior now proved, he was just a commodity to Coach Walton, who did not really care about all that other stuff he had been saying to Avery for the past several months.

Then, in week eight of the season, when East Devlin was set to go up against their arch-rival, Coach Walton reached back out to Avery. Avery came into Coach's classroom a bit confused, as there was no way he was getting a recruiting pitch during the eighth week of the season. Coach Walton said to him, "I saw your name on the D/F report. You are spending your lunches with me until your name is not on there anymore."

Avery was a good student and had really messed up on only one big assignment. He was not slipping, nor was anything of outside influence bringing him down. But he gained a lot of trust in Coach Walton at that moment. After four lunches together, Avery's grade had shot back up to a B, and he was no longer requested in Coach Walton's room for lunch. As Avery was walking out of the room, Coach Walton thought he would give one more try by telling Avery he wished he was suiting up for him this Friday.

Avery, always the skeptic, asked why. Coach said what he typically did and talked about the virtues of football helping Avery grow into a man. But then, he chuckled and told Avery how much he would help against the press man-to-man defense their rival liked to play against outside receivers. In that moment of honesty, coupled with Coach Walton caring about his grades, Avery decided to play the next season.

The season went well. But that did not mean that Avery did not still have anxiety about playing. He later confided to Coach Walton that he had a terrible experience with a previous coach. Coach kept this in mind at all times and dealt with the quirks that came with Avery. For example, he always asked about contingency plans and worst-case scenarios. Coach knew this impacted the rest of the team, so he and Avery agreed to go over these together before school. This allowed both of them to have success.

They fell into a nice rhythm as a coach-athlete team and as a collective overall team. In fact, by mid-season, the only thing that drew any additional attention to Avery as part of the team was his pre-game jitters. Avery would spend considerable time alone and with a bucket prior to the start of each game. Coach knew that the jitters did not subside for Avery until he got into the flow of the game. As a result, Avery was almost always the target of a play during the first series.

As Coach Walton continued to learn about his players, he continued to adjust. He did what he needed to do in order to get the most out of his athletes, instead of simply expecting them to conform to strategies and tactics that made him comfortable.

CHAPTER 8

Description of an Enneagram Type 6

An Enneagram Type 6 is also known as "the Loyal Skeptic." Loyal Skeptics believe that the world is inherently dangerous and that they can't possibly survive it all on their own. Thus they look for consistency and security in groups and leadership figures, and once they find their group or leader, they become fiercely committed to them.

Loyal Skeptics are inquisitive, reliable, hard-working, and trustworthy. They make great troubleshooters because they have a constant "the sky is falling" attitude that keeps them on the lookout for the *bad thing* that is about to happen at any given moment. This hyper-focus on what could go wrong makes them invaluable when a team or organization is looking to make a change in procedure or philosophy. Very naturally, and almost always, they can play devil's advocate when any new idea or change is being introduced.

Type 6s can see all the ways in which things can go wrong, preparing the head coach or CEO for the pitfalls ahead. The downside of this constant worry is that it causes Type 6s to freeze or procrastinate at decision time. When a person only sees the downside of every decision, it is hard for them to pull the trigger. Additionally, they can feel dismissed by others who do not see the world as a risk-mitigation exercise and do not heed their cautionary tales, leading to fractured professional and personal relationships.

Triad

As part of the Fear Triad, Type 6s internalize their fear into crushing anxiety that is constantly with them. Fear is caused by a clear and present danger, such as a car swerving into your lane. Anxiety, however, is felt as a sense of apprehension from an unknown or potential danger that may or may not ever materialize. Type 6s spend the majority of their time living in their head asking the questions, "What might go wrong?" or "How is this going to get screwed up today?"

Type 6s can make up a scenario causing worry even if there is nothing of concern from a pragmatic perspective. Despite the propensity for anxiety and strong allegiance to the status quo, Type 6s are considered the most dependable of all the Enneagram types, as their desire for security and strength in numbers makes them great teammates. They are the glue that holds relationships, teams, and organizations together, and they will stick with a trusted organization or leader through thick and thin.

Comparison to Other Types in the Fear/Head Triad

Fear in this triad can be compared to a rumor. Type 5s understand that the rumor exists but want to repress it so badly that they may move to another town so as to not have to engage with it. Type 7s understand the rumor exists but choose to numb themselves to the rumor and distract themselves with any other activity that can occupy their mind. Type 6s are scared of the rumor and must express this fear, sharing their feelings with anyone who will listen.

Motivations

Enneagram Type 6s are motivated by the need for security and support. Their predisposition is to seek out groups or communities that can provide both. They are called the Loyal Skeptics because they will stay loyal no matter what, so they won't be abandoned in this cruel world.

While they are quick to point out potential pitfalls, Type 6s do not have confidence in their own abilities and decision-making. This leads to an intense commitment to the group and the desire to "go down with the ship" rather than leave the group. The risk of leaving and needing to fight through life on their own is substantially scarier to a Type 6 than a grandiose failure.

As a result, a team full of Type 6s led by a strong and competent leader is a tough team to beat. Each person feels responsible for the one beside them, so they work hard to protect each other. An issue occurs if, and when, leadership breaks down or is absent in a key moment, and the Type 6 has to take charge or make a decision. Frequently, in this situation, Type 6s are unable to see a path to success through all the landmines. As a result, the fearful Type 6 will abandon the campaign and look for someone or something to blame.

Fear

The basic fear of a Type 6 is to be without support and stability. This fear is expressed most in the inability of Type 6s to make decisions. This manifests in a Type 6 not having the confidence to trust in their own thinking or judgments. Thus, they have the tendency to defer to others to make their decisions for them, but only after warning them of the potential downside of their decision.

Operating life through this paradigm tends to lead to negative consequences resulting in an unhealthy Type 6 spiraling into the fear of being all on their own. This fear also makes it virtually impossible for Type 6s to leave bad situations, and they will stay a part of horrible relationships, jobs, and teams for the simple reason that they don't think they can navigate this dangerous world on their own.

Craving

Type 6s crave security. Unfortunately, for Type 6s, this craving is essentially insatiable. Due to their never-ending questioning of what might go wrong, they are forever on the lookout for people, places, and things that will provide the security they desire. Until they can come to trust their own inner guidance and gut feelings, they will constantly be on the lookout for what influence, group, or person can provide the most certainty and never settle into a comfortable environment.

Surprisingly, as much as they have a hard time making decisions, Type 6s resist others making decisions for them. They do not want to be controlled, but they also don't want to take any responsibility that might put them in life's crosshairs. Toggling back and forth between these two guiding principles causes Type 6s to freeze when life demands a choice. This is when the security network they have built comes in handy.

Self-Sabotage

The motivation, fear, and craving of the Enneagram Type 6 manifest in self-sabotaging behavior when a Type 6 is operating on autopilot and does not recognize that their desire for safety and security can serve to push people away. As a result of always doubting and questioning every decision, Type 6s can drive away healthy relationships. Conversely, their desire for security can lead them to stay in unhealthy relationships or situations. Both situations present Type 6s with a lack of true security, and, as a result, they have self-sabotaged themselves out of their basic desire.

Additionally, Type 6s are missing important opportunities in their lives due to their inability to make their own decisions and trust their own thoughts. This is most often expressed in the Type 6's debilitating procrastination. The lack of their ability to pull the trigger and make a choice leaves the Type 6 stuck watching the world pass them by. Instead of growing and moving forward, they retreat to their secure and comfortable groups to lament all the "bad luck" that befalls them. Or they become angry and make a laundry list of all their accomplishments that have yet to be rewarded.

Role on a Team
Type 6s will position themselves in the "pack" of the team. They make terrific teammates because they will do whatever is asked and don't require any attention or spotlight to shine on them. They are just fine with sharing in the accolades of the team's success. Ideally, they will shine when placed in a position where they have a well-defined task and aren't asked to make too many leadership decisions. They truly are the glue that holds a team together. They will embrace and support strong leadership, as long as that leadership provides trust and security. Type 6s do not perform well under heavy-handed authoritarian leadership. This will cause them to shut down, at best, and rebel, at worst.

Continuum of Behaviors
Every Enneagram type has default behaviors but also a predisposition to behave in different ways depending upon their emotional and behavioral health. When healthy, Type 6s behave like Enneagram Type 9s; and when under stress, they typically behave like Enneagram Type 3s.

Healthy
Type 6s, who can be fearful and pessimistic, become more optimistic and relaxed like Type 9s.

CHAPTER 8

THE ENNEAGRAM

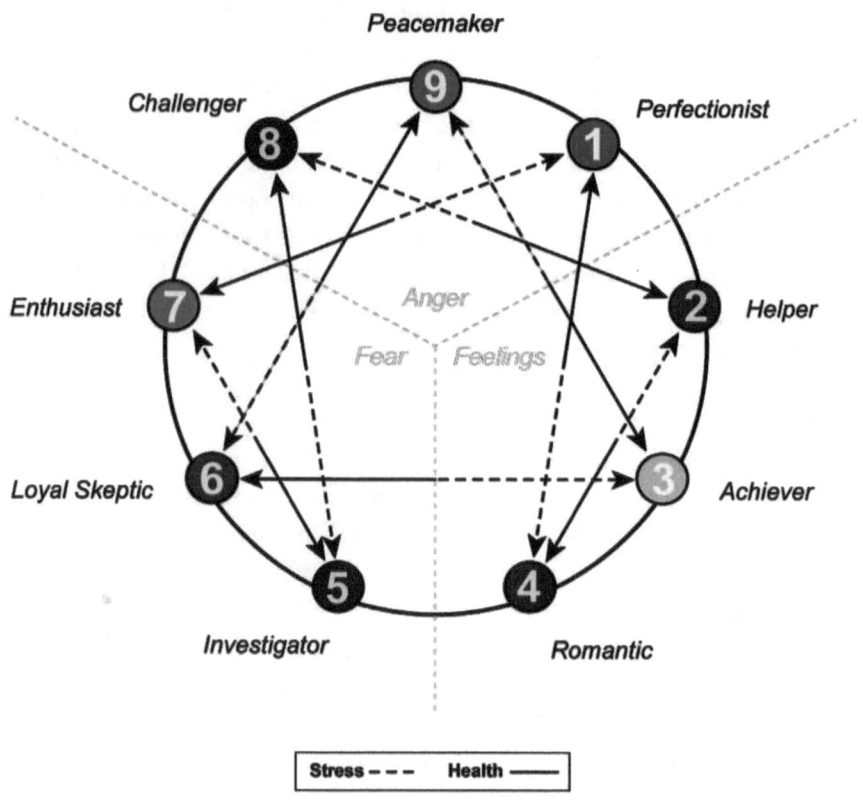

Stress

Type 6s, who are dutiful and loyal, become competitive and arrogant, like Type 3s.

Same, But Different—Enneagram Wings

Although there are nine basic personality types in the Enneagram, each type can be influenced by the types on either side, making two people of the same Enneagram type appear very different. In the case of Type 6s, they can either lean toward Type 5 or Type 7.

Type 6s with a 5-wing tend to be more intellectual, cautious, and self-controlled. They will gravitate toward a defined belief system or a group that shares their values and ideals. Less social than the typical Type 6, they protect their privacy and recharge their batteries with alone time.

Type 6s with a 7-wing tend to be more adventurous, entertaining, and enthusiastic. They are less risk averse, choosing to put themselves in harm's way by making their own decisions but being aware enough of the risk to keep a backup plan in case things don't work out. This increased ability to make decisions can push this type up to a leadership role if the situation calls for it.

I might be an Enneagram Type 6 if . . .

- When things are going well in my life or in my relationship, I often wonder what is going to happen to ruin it.
- I have been called the devil's advocate many times in my life.
- I have a hard time finishing tasks because I can't decide what to do next.
- When I start to worry about something, it is hard for me not to obsess about it.
- I constantly question whether or not I am making the right decisions, particularly when it comes to safety and security.
- When faced with the unknown, I am told I can be very pessimistic.
- I prefer to be in the company of others. I drown in my own thoughts of what might go wrong when I have too much alone time.
- I often procrastinate when given tasks with no timeline or direction.
- I have numerous friends but only a few that I trust completely.
- I add value to the teams or relationships I am in by helping others see the potential pitfalls in the plans they are making.
- When forced to make a decision, I'll always choose the one that is the safest even if it costs me a great opportunity.

- I often ask for guidance but tend to ignore the advice because I don't trust it and don't want to be controlled.
- I am slow to trust others, particularly leaders. Once they have earned my trust, however, I am loyal to a fault.

R^3

Bobby Flynn and Sam Berg were best friends, teammates, and co-captains on the perennial powerhouse boys' lacrosse team at West Central High in Ohio. Both played as attackers and seemed to have some sort of ESP, always knowing where the other was on the field. Bobby was the natural leader of the two and would run the offense, calling out plays and keeping everyone moving in the proper direction. Sam was the "glue" guy of the team. He worked hard, did whatever the team needed, and supported his teammates. For a coach, it was a match made in heaven.

Coach Curtis had been the head lacrosse coach for twenty-five years and had built West Central into what it was today. He was a tough coach that demanded a lot from his players. It wasn't unusual to see him in an apoplectic state on the sidelines encouraging his best players to play harder. Bobby ate that up and took the brunt of Coach Curtis's harsh critiques and communication style.

This worked for Bobby, and he would then relay a less aggressive and direct form of the same message to Sam and the rest of the team. Sam would make sure everyone was on the same page, then put in the dirty work to make sure the play/plan worked.

This is the way the team functioned for three years, producing deeper and deeper runs into the state series, culminating with a berth in the semifinals during their junior season. Heading into Sam and Bobby's senior year, the expectations were high, to say the least. They had almost every player from last season back, and another solid group of underclassmen was waiting in the wings. This could be the year that they added another trophy to the case.

The season started like many before. Bobby and Sam were as sharp as ever. Coach Curtis continued his usual colorful sideline antics that seemed to push the team to even greater heights.

For the first few games, it was as if Bobby and Sam were operating with one brain on the field. They were the personification of synergy. Both players complemented and amplified each other's skills perfectly.

Then, everything ground to a halt.

They were in a tough physical game with a nearby school. The score was tied, and time was running out. Sam hit Bobby in stride as he cut to the goal and pulled back a shot. Right as he released the ball toward the net, he was body-checked hard and crumpled to the ground, clutching his right knee. The ball hit the back of the net as the final horn sounded. West Central had won, but nobody was celebrating. Everyone was looking at Bobby lying on the ground, waiting for him to bounce back up.

The seconds passed like hours until finally Bobby gingerly got up, refusing any help. He limped to the sidelines, and the crowd erupted in applause as a collective sigh of relief could practically be heard. Bobby knew that sigh of relief was misguided. He suspected his knee was badly hurt, and the following week, an MRI confirmed what he already knew.

Bobby's season was over.

Coach Curtis, not one to dwell on the bad breaks of the game, pulled the team together before practice after he got the report and told everyone the bad news. He looked straight at Sam and told him he would have to take Bobby's role as the team leader. Coach made no public mention of what Bobby was going through or how much he meant to the team. Coach kept it simple.

As Coach continued on with his next "man up" speech, Sam looked around at all the eyes staring at him, put his head down, and physically took a couple of steps back. It looked like he'd just seen a ghost. The normally talkative and supportive teammate that Sam had been, disappeared. When Coach called on him to step up, he stepped back. Literally and metaphorically. When the team made it to the field for practice, it seemed as if he was just going through the motions.

The next game didn't look much different from practice. Sam "played scared" to quote Coach Curtis, who was already losing whatever patience he had left. The sharp, aggressive passes that Sam had once fired to Bobby were replaced with hesitation and Sam pulling the ball back out of the zone to start over.

CHAPTER 8

Coach Curtis had seen enough and called timeout to motivate his one remaining star player. But, motivation to Coach Curtis looked a lot like chastising Sam to many others. Though he spent the entire time yelling at the entire team, it was obvious that the tirade was directed at Sam.

The good old-fashioned butt-chewing that took place during the timeout led to a change in Sam's behavior; unfortunately, Sam started playing more and more tentatively. This led to Coach Curtis pushing harder and harder. The season was in a negative spiral, and it seemed both Coach and Sam were either incapable or unwilling to adapt their behaviors.

West Central dropped that game. And the next. And the next. Sam was a shell of himself. His body language was horrible, and his play matched. In conversations with his family and teammates, he began blaming his coach. The culture that had been building to a crescendo over three-plus years was crumbling in just a matter of weeks.

The season was slipping away, and Coach Curtis had no answers.

Review
Coach Curtis needed to take a step back and review this scenario from the perspective of the Enneagram. Sam was a classic Type 6. When paired with a great leader, Type 6s can help a team achieve great things by being a great hard-working teammate. However, Type 6s begin to struggle as soon as they are thrust into the leadership role. This struggle is compounded when this new responsibility is given unexpectedly and without great support around them. Moreover, Type 6s do not thrive under the direct leadership of a very authoritarian leader.

Reset
Coach Curtis needed to recognize that Sam and Bobby were very different people and would respond best to different leadership styles. Yelling and screaming may motivate some Enneagram types, and be tolerated by others, but will totally shrink a Type 6.

Type 6s do not do well with that type of leadership and motivation. When first presented with this evidence, instead of backing off and adjusting, Coach Curtis pushed harder. As a coach and leader, just because a tactic has worked in the past with other players does not mean it will always work. In the same way that great coaches adjust their game plans and strategy based on the talent of the team, they should adjust their behavior and the way they manage their athletes. A reset would have provided Coach Curtis with this perspective.

Resolve
In this scenario, Coach Curtis could have resolved Sam's anxiety, nervousness, and uncertainty in a variety of ways. The easiest fix would have been by toning down the gruff behavior and direct communication style. Sam's success was dependent upon him feeling like he was supported and safe to make mistakes.

It would have also helped if Coach Curtis would have acknowledged the loss of Bobby. Sam needed to feel humanized instead of being made to feel like a cog in the machine. Type 6s need to know that they are going to be loved and secure, no matter what happens. When this reassurance does not take place, they doubt the loyalty given to them and, therefore, start to rescind some of the loyalty they have granted the other person.

As has been said repeatedly, Type 6s are incredible assets to any team, with incredible leadership potential. While Type 6s often imagine the worst-case scenario in any situation, this can also be a superpower. They are incredibly loyal and hard-working given the right leadership and circumstances.

While all Enneagram types have the capacity to be amazing leaders, Type 6s are not natural leaders. For success, they need to be surrounded by supportive coaches or administrators who prioritize teamwork and are committed to a process. Type 6s believe in doing the right work, in the right way, and that the data (winning, losing, etc.) will take care of itself.

Coach Curtis's inability to soften his tone and let Sam know that he was in his corner drove Sam to shut down from fear and anxiety. When there is no clear support and a core feeling of psychological safety for a Type 6, they will default to their autopilot behavior. In this case, it led to Sam shutting down in order to protect himself from judgment and potential failure.

Tomorrow Takeaways

- Review the past month and write down each scenario where you were faced with fear or anxiety. For each instance, ask yourself, "Were my feelings real or imagined?" Then analyze how many times this imagined fear (anxiety) has taken away opportunities for yourself and your team.

- Grab a notebook, and for the next week, write down each time your mind drifts toward the negative or what might go wrong. How does this type of daydreaming stifle your work and creativity? How does it contribute to your procrastination?

- Ask a close friend, family member, or colleague to identify when you are seemingly making a simple situation into a much more complex endeavor. Identify if that helps you in any way.

- Evaluate your relationships and your groups. How many of these are not serving you anymore? Why are you still clinging to them? How would your life open up if you got rid of them?

- Create more space in your life for growth by making a list of all the tasks you need to finish, putting them in order of importance, and giving yourself a timeline of when each needs to be finished. Most importantly, do not take on any more tasks until each one of these is completed.

- Analyze whether you bring energy or drain energy from groups and teams you participate in or with.

CHAPTER 9

Type 7 Deep Dive

COACH GATES WAS IN HER TWENTY-NINTH YEAR OF COACHING VOLLEYball at Fuller High School. She had developed quite the resume over this time. Coach had won two state championships and nine regional championships and had helped produce twelve Division I athletes. She was a local legend, with four years left before retirement from both the classroom and the bench.

Even with her decorated resume, Coach Gates was about to decide that she had only made three other times in her career. She was about to name Jacqueline Johns the starting setter as a freshman. She had been coaching long enough to know that placing this type of recognition and responsibility on a fourteen-year-old meant that she had to have more than just talent.

Jacqueline had some of that "it" factor that is so hard to quantify. She had a way about her that allowed her to fit in with the older girls without seeking attention in a negative way. She was so full of energy, so extroverted, and simply enthusiastic about life—not just volleyball.

As had been Coach Gates's process for over a decade, she had one athlete from each grade level sit on an advisory for the program. Coach Gates found that giving a group of young women control over some aspects of the program and practice helped create ownership and allowed for more people to lead within the program than just the coaches and captains.

Jacqueline immediately demonstrated her value in this advisory, even as a ninth grader. She was not shy, and she spoke her mind. She had so many new and innovative ideas that, at times, it could be hard to keep up with her. The group came to a consensus on the value of many of these new ideas, and different games and competitions became a regular part of practice.

After six weeks of summer practice and preseason work, Jacqueline had fit right in and Coach Gates had zero reservations about making her a varsity starter. It was not until week four of the competitive season that Coach started to have some significant concerns.

First, the advisory was making some atypical recommendations. Jacqueline, as such a skilled and extroverted communicator, became the unnamed leader of the advisory as a ninth grader. This was not the problem, though. The problem was that the athlete advisory continued to recommend changes, creating disruptions to any type of established practice structure or routine. They continued to come to Coach with a new drill or warm-up that they saw on social media and wanted to deviate from the typical practice structure.

Understandably, Coach did not heed all of the advice given by the advisory. This did not outwardly frustrate the group, but it intensified the call for changes from the advisory. It was as if the more Coach said no, the more Jacqueline was able to convince the group to recommend different changes.

Then, an issue that Coach had noticed in out-of-conference play became very evident in a game against perennial conference powerhouse St. Albert's High School. During practice, Coach Gates taught the team that St. Albert's weakness would be off of the one-set. A one-set in volleyball is a quick set to the middle of the net for a kill.

After one set it was clear that Coach Gates's scouting of St. Albert's was correct, as Fuller convincingly won set number one. Then, in set number two, Jacqueline quit using the one-set. Nothing had changed. The lineups were the same. The game flow was the same. The coaching plan had not deviated. Only Jacqueline had changed.

The issue was that the other sets being used were not proving effective. In fact, St. Albert's won set two. Coach Gates reminded the entire team of the scouting report, but she did so while looking Jacqueline directly in the eyes. Set three began, and Jacqueline continued to set, seemingly, wherever she wanted, without acquiescing to Coach Gates's wishes.

Coach Gates called a timeout. While the whole team was listening, Coach Gates was going to do something she seldom did in her long career. She simply talked to one player during the timeout. She called out Jacqueline for not following the game plan. Jacqueline sat in silence. Coach demanded an answer for why she quit following the plan that was working.

Eventually, Jacqueline admitted that continuing to use the one-set was boring. Coach Gates asked a firm, but fair question. "Jacqueline, do you want to win or be entertained?" While Jacqueline did not like being confronted, having her priorities made clear for her helped her to change her behavior. Jacqueline started using the one-set again, and the team won in three sets.

This interaction on the sidelines helped to give Coach Gates a keen insight into what was happening with advisory, as well. She was able to pull Jacqueline in and discuss her leadership in private. Coach was able to articulate that the advisory was meant to help the program and while it was in part designed to give her insight to keep them from stagnation, its ultimate goal is to produce a better program.

Through the conversation, it became clear to Jacqueline (for the first time) that she was looking for things that were cool or fun, and not things that she actually thought would benefit the program. Coach Gates also helped her to understand that some people thrive on routine, even if she finds it boring. Thus, as a leader, she needed to balance her desire for new and innovative practices with those that would help the entire team and program move forward—not just meet her own personal needs.

Throughout the next three years, Coach Gates and Jacqueline continued to have a productive relationship. Coach realized that Jacqueline needed something new and different to stay engaged. Jacqueline realized that new and different was not always the best path forward for the program. Together, they helped each other, and the program continued to have success in the final years of Coach Gates's career.

Description of Enneagram Type 7

An Enneagram Type 7 is also known as "the Enthusiast." Enthusiasts believe that their sole purpose is to squeeze every drop of juice out of life. They are optimistic, spontaneous, adventurous, and always looking for the next big thing. They are the life of the party and the perfect person to go on an adventure with.

The minds of Type 7s are able to rapidly move from one idea or topic to the next, making them great forward thinkers willing to push the envelope of what is possible. The converse is that seldom can Type 7s stay committed to one task long enough to see it through to completion. Type 7s thrive in roles where they can be the "idea" person.

However, all of this idea generation and spontaneity comes at a cost. Type 7s get distracted easily and have trouble seeing their ideas through to completion. In a nutshell, they are excellent starters but terrible finishers. Thus, Type 7s who ascend to leadership roles must be paired with a great executor, who can see the job to completion while their Type 7 counterparts are moving on to the next thing.

Triad

As part of the Fear Triad, Type 7s will do anything to avoid, ignore, or outrun their fear. The fast-paced and frequently erratic behavior of Type 7s can best be visualized as someone running away from an avalanche as the snow (or their fears) continues to close in on them.

Type 7s feel compelled to keep moving to avoid the monotony, challenges, and pain of life. They also are the type best described by permanent FOMO (Fear of Missing Out). It is deeper than typical FOMO, however. Type 7s are afraid if stagnant, they will be forced to confront all the pain and discomfort they are fighting so hard to ignore. As a result, they are on a never-ending quest to keep moving.

Type 7s typically do not want to be attached to a singular choice, and, as a result, they struggle with making decisions. This is not limited to major life choices; it also applies to seemingly innocuous day-to-day decisions. Type 7s will take longer when ordering at a restaurant, ask for multiple substitutions to items on the menu, and tend to take longer when shopping than all of the other types. Getting a Type 7 to commit to anything is a monumental task.

Comparison to Other Types in the Fear/Head Triad
Fear in this triad can be compared to a rumor. Type 5s understand that the rumor exists but want to repress it so badly that they may move to another town so as to not have to engage with it. Type 6s are scared of the rumor but must express this fear and share their feelings with anyone who will listen. Type 7s, however, understand that the rumor exists but choose to numb themselves to the rumor and distract themselves with any other activity that can occupy their mind.

Motivations
Enneagram Type 7s are motivated by the need to plan and experience pleasurable and exciting events and challenges. This core motivation, combined with their enthusiasm, charisma, and outgoing personality, make Type 7s the kind of people everyone wants to be around. As a result, Type 7s will typically ascend quickly to leadership roles or, at minimum, popularity, in a group setting, and can foster a lot of excitement and change for a team or organization.

However, Type 7s can quickly lose influence as a leader or a coach. As a group tries to keep up with the incredible amount of energy their leader expends and new ideas they create, stress and exhaustion often present themselves. This typically manifests in a state of overwhelm for the group, as most people can't continue with the rapid change in direction. Thus, a Type 7 can wear out their welcome as quickly as they rose to power and influence.

Fear
The basic fear of a Type 7 is of pain and confronting reality. The basic proposition that guides their life is that if they continue to focus on new experiences and think about the future, they can continue to ignore or avoid the pain in their life. Thus, the fear of stagnation and "feeling" reality drives the frenetic behavior of Type 7s.

If a Type 7 can keep their mind busy enough, they will never have to face or even acknowledge the fear and pain they have inside; so, the Type 7 is on an eternal quest for the next fun ride, adventurous vacation, big idea, or new experience.

To describe this at a deeper level, as long as Type 7s are still on the ride, they won't have to come to grips with their reality. That reality is that deep down they don't know what their purpose is or how to make the right choices to discover what their true purpose is. This lack of trust in their own abilities, coupled with the emptiness of a life without direction, drives them to find anything that will keep their mind occupied and away from this realization.

Craving

Type 7s crave freedom. This may be freedom from control, boredom, monotony, or from anything else that will cause them to slow down. This desire for freedom results in a gluttonous approach to life.

This thirst for freedom makes Type 7s the least risk-averse of all the Enneagram types. Nothing, not even risk, is as important as being able to live life on your own terms, free from guilt and regret. As a result, this may lead a Type 7 coach to try a new play they found at a clinic, instead of doing something much more likely to work. The rush from pushing forward and trying something new, despite the risk, is worth giving up the potential reward of the status quo for a Type 7.

A Type 7's ability to jump quickly from one thing to the next doesn't just end with experiences. They are also able to change directions on a whim if things are becoming too real or they make the wrong decisions. This ability to transition so quickly leads to Type 7s having no attachment to the outcomes of their choices. This puts a massive strain on their relationships, jobs, health, and finances, which can ultimately lead to more dangerous behavior or reliance on substances for their next big ride.

Self-Sabotage

The motivation, fear, and craving of the Enneagram Type 7 manifests in self-sabotaging behavior when a Type 7 is operating on autopilot and does not recognize that they are so focused on their journey that they have no idea what their destination is. Moreover, they take so much time focusing on what is next, they miss out on enjoying the present. If a Type 7 buys a beautiful new house instead of enjoying it, they will focus on the first big renovation project that may not even be necessary.

Type 7s become so wrapped up in variety and fun that everything takes a back seat, including those they share their life with. Their relationships fall apart, as no one wants to play second fiddle to every wild idea you have. As a financial partner, Type 7s are very difficult to live and work with as there is always a next adventure that needs to occur, whatever the price.

Trust is the key ingredient of any good relationship. It is very hard to trust someone that doesn't come through for you or show up when they are supposed to. This type of behavior is typical of a Type 7 acting on autopilot because they have moved on to the next idea and struggle to put anyone else's ideas, feelings, or priorities first in their life. As their relationships and professional stature fall apart, instead of self-correcting the behavior, Type 7s revert even more to their autopilot behavior and push even harder for the next rush of experience or opportunity, until they end up alone.

Role on a Team

With their charisma and extroversion, Type 7s will quickly ascend to either leadership or some highly visible role on most teams. As leaders, Type 7s' enthusiasm for the moment makes them highly skilled motivators pushing the team to new heights. Their constant focus on the new idea or scheme to win the game helps them be great innovators and makes them a nightmare to game plan against as they seem to never create tendencies. However, sustained success for the Type 7 as a leader requires surrounding themselves with people that will carry out their vision and finish the job. Additionally, Type 7s need someone to check their desire to explore new or different ideas or concepts. As a head coach, a Type 7 needs someone who is willing to help them recognize their autopilot behaviors as a potential detriment to overall success.

As players, Type 7s flourish in systems where they are given some freedom to freelance and have fun. Changing up the practice routine or

CHAPTER 9

keeping them on their toes with new drills are musts. Failure to do so will cause Type 7s to check out at best, and rebel, at worst. Type 7s are also the most likely to mention transferring when things get monotonous or even discuss playing a different sport in the same season, just to add some spice to their lives. When coaching Type 7s, it is imperative to keep things interesting for them but to also continually re-recruit them to the team they are already a part of.

Continuum of Behaviors

Every Enneagram type has default behaviors but also a predisposition to behave in different ways depending upon their emotional and behavioral

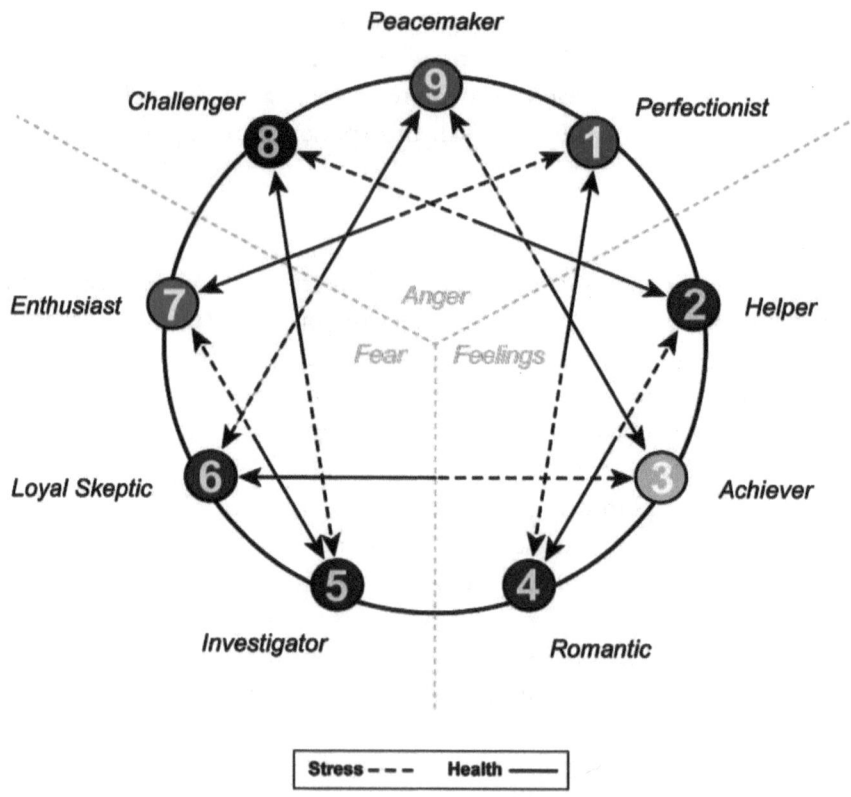

health. When healthy, Type 7s behave like Enneagram Type 5s; and when under stress, they typically behave like Enneagram Type 1s.

Healthy
Type 7s, who can be erratic and risk-taking, become more focused and controlled, like a Type 5.

Stress
Type 7s, who are flexible and optimistic, become rigid and pessimistic, like a Type 1.

Same, But Different—Enneagram Wings
Although there are nine basic personality types in the Enneagram, each type can be influenced by the types on either side, making two people of the same Enneagram type appear very different. In the case of Type 7s, they can either lean toward Type 6 or Type 8.

Type 7s with a 6-wing tend to be less concerned about experiences and give more time and attention to relationships and projects. They are still motivated to experience all the fun life has to offer, but they are more diligent at cultivating relationships and finishing tasks.

Type 7s with an 8-wing tend to be extremely competitive, aggressive, and bold. Where average 7s tend to change whimsically if things don't go their way, this type of 7 will force things to go their way. While the rush of starting a new endeavor or coming up with a new idea is their driving force, they don't have the time, nor the patience to wait for its completion. This type of 7 will rebel or fight any type of rules or control that they disagree with.

I might be an Enneagram Type 7 if . . .
- I have a hard time finishing things. When I get into a project, I start thinking about what I should do next and just move on to it.
- I am always ready for a fun, last-minute adventure. Heck, life is one big adventure!
- I quickly get bored with routine and love to try new things.

- I resist committing to things and making hard decisions. I often ask why I can't just do it all or have it exactly my way, even if that does not initially appear as an option.
- I am constantly wondering what I am missing out on (FOMO) when I am engaged in something.
- I am eternally optimistic, never even considering what challenges might await.
- I avoid most serious conversations, and if they move in that direction, I'll lighten the mood with a joke or quickly change the topic.
- I tend to push back or ignore anyone or anything trying to tell me what to do.
- I find that the anticipation of something is often far more exciting than actually doing it.
- I don't care for expectations. Just let me be me.
- I would rather make a bad decision or something counterproductive to my goals than remain bored.

R^3

Ashley Grover was one of the best athletes that the state of California had ever produced. From the time she was a freshman at Washington High School in northern California, she excelled in any sport she tried. And much to the chagrin of the competition, and her coaches, she tried them all.

As a freshman, she was the starting libero on a varsity team that made it all the way to the sectional finals. Later that year, she was the leadoff leg of the 4x400 relay team that placed fifth at the state track meet.

In her sophomore year, she decided to try cross country instead of volleyball and helped the team make its first-ever trip to the state meet. Over the winter, she tried her hand at basketball, where she was the starting point guard and made all-conference honorable mention. When spring rolled around, everyone assumed she would run track again since all four members of her relay team were back, and they had a chance to break the school record that had stood for over twenty years.

Ashley had other ideas. She shocked everyone and decided to play soccer.

Coach Meyer was in her fourth year leading the girls' soccer program at Washington. When she took over the program, Washington was the perennial bottom-dweller of the conference. Before Coach Meyer came to town, the program had never had a winning season. Coach Meyer was a competitor and an incredible athlete herself. She was a former D-1 star defender and was determined to turn the program around.

By year three, Coach Meyer had guided the program to its first .500 season in school history. The team was very young, and there was a buzz around the program for her fourth season. Needless to say, finding out that Ashley was coming out for the team had Coach Meyer and the town thinking about what might be.

Coach Meyer had not had much interaction with Ashley prior to her announcing that she would be playing soccer. Ashley had never shown much interest in soccer and never came to any of the youth camps Coach Meyer had held when Ashley was in junior high. All she knew was what she had heard about Ashley—she was an incredible athlete, a bundle of energy, and loved by her teammates. The only negative was from the other coaches complaining that she never stuck with a sport long enough to really make an impact.

From the first practice, Coach Meyer knew she had something special in Ashley. She was far and away the best athlete on the team and seemed to pick up skills without much effort. Being a defensive star, Coach Meyer had been tinkering with a new defensive strategy that could stifle opponents and put Washington over the top.

Coming into the season, Coach knew they had talented forwards that could score from anywhere. The missing link was the right kind of athlete to run the defensive system Coach Meyer wanted to deploy, and Ashley was the perfect fit.

It took all of about three practices for Coach Meyer to insert Ashley into the middle defender position and begin to teach her the nuances of the position. She took to it like a fish to water. After their first few preseason scrimmages, it was clear that this team had all the potential to be special. In her first three years, scoring had never been the problem;

they could put up goals on anyone. The problem was that they gave up goals just as fast as they scored them. With Ashley running point on her defensive strategy, she knew they finally had a complete team.

The season started as Coach Meyer had envisioned. Their defense was suffocating their opponents, and the offense was scoring goals in bunches. Best of all, the kids were having a ton of fun. Ashley brought incredible energy and was always pushing for something new at practice.

The veterans on the team once told Coach Meyer that somehow, Ashley made even conditioning drills fun. While profoundly silly, she really drew the team closer together by getting them to wear a different pair of goofy socks to every game. The season was going incredibly well, and aside from the occasional hiccup resulting from Ashley getting out of position, which led to great scoring chances for the other team, everything was going as planned.

At the halfway point of the season, Washington was ten and two, almost matching their win total from the year before. However, Coach Meyer knew that the second half of the season was going to be much tougher. She was right, and the team dropped two of their next three games.

Each loss was a heartbreaking one-goal defeat. Coach Meyer had experienced her share of one-goal defeats as both player and coach, and normally did not get too worked up by such outcomes, but this year was different. The girls were playing hard; however, they were giving up silly goals that cost them games.

The new defense wasn't the problem. The problem was that Ashley would leave her position to go after balls that were not her responsibility. During the last game, she spent most of the second half on the wrong end of the field playing with the forwards. She scored a goal, but the defense gave up three as a result of Ashley being out of position.

Coach Meyer worked with Ashley, reiterating the importance of her being the attack point of the defense. Ashley took it all in, seemed to understand, and played the position hard for a few minutes, but would then wander upfield as play moved in that direction. The team was still playing well, but they were losing games they had no business losing simply due to sloppy play on defense.

The harder Coach Meyer pushed on Ashley, the more Ashley would push back and play out of position. She argued that she could do both—score goals and play defense.

Finally, Coach Meyer had enough. Not only was Ashley openly defying her, but the team was growing frustrated that she was constantly out of position. The energy that Ashley once brought to the team was the same energy she was now draining from them.

The season was slipping away from Coach Meyer and her team. She continued to push, teach, and reiterate the discipline necessary to be a great defender. Ashley continued to seem as though she understood but chose not to execute. This led to less and less playing time for Ashley and less success for the team.

The season stumbled to a close with yet another 13–13 record and no true forward movement for the program, despite the infusion of talent and athleticism.

Review
Coach Meyer needed to step back from the situation and view Ashley through the lens of the Enneagram. Ashley was clearly a Type 7, who was rebelling against the direction she was being given, simply out of boredom. The constant need for new and stimulating experiences overrode any sense of responsibility or necessary discipline required to play two forty-minute halves of high school soccer. Being the middle defender was not enough for her. Ashley *needed* to be in the action.

Reset
In this scenario, Coach Meyer was doing what most coaches do when confronted with an athlete who is not playing within their defined role. She began disciplining Ashley more and more, culminating in reducing her playing time. For any Type 7, this would result in more rebellion and disconnection from the team.

With the tools provided by Enneagram, if Coach Meyer would have taken a minute to deeply assess the situation, she would have discovered that there was another way to move forward. She would have individualized and customized her coaching to bring the most out of Ashley, and to keep the team moving forward.

Resolve

The resolution in this situation would have required Coach Meyer to adjust her typical approach of playing athletes in a singular position and find ways to get Ashley involved in other ways. Giving Ashley twelve minutes a half at forward would have given her the thrill and stimulation of playing all over the field and would have ensured that the middle defender position was filled at all times.

Ashley's main position could be playing the point on defense, but for small chunks of the game, giving her a taste of other positions would have led to increased discipline in each area. The increased stimulation would have led to increased focus and quelled the ever-present FOMO Ashley felt by being "stuck" as a defender for ninety minutes per game.

Type 7s are typically talented individuals that have a wide range of skill sets. They are sometimes both the greatest and the most frustrating assets on a team. Their unquenchable thirst for stimulation and variety will lead them to rebel against any authority that tries to pigeonhole them into a static position. However, the same motivations help them bring energy and fun to almost every situation, and they often show great creativity in how they play the game as well.

When coaching Type 7s, it is imperative to find creative ways to move their bodies and stimulate their minds. This intentional stimulation strategically provided by the coach should keep them engaged in the game or process but also maximize their incredible potential.

Keep in mind that Type 7s have an innate ability to keep teams loose by getting everyone to have fun. Having them in an advisory role can be very beneficial, as long as the coach can keep them focused on what is best for the team and not simply what they personally find fun. Type 7s, unmitigated, can be consumed with finding activities that keep them busy and satisfy their own needs.

Tomorrow Takeaways

- Always looking for the next opportunity, you fail to see how completing the opportunity you just started will lead to something bigger. Analyze the past six months and identify how many opportunities you have lost in the pursuit of the next best thing. What would happen in your personal and professional life if you saw more things to completion?

- Exercise daily to burn off all of your excess energy. Renewed focus on your health will ultimately lead to you being able to explore more opportunities in the future.

- Identify the circumstances in your life that make you pull back, avoid, or rebel against. What do these have in common? What are you trying to avoid? How would confronting these issues release you to experience more of life?

- Begin a practice of daily meditation. A more focused mind will lead to greater outcomes for all of your grand ideas.

- Create a gratitude journal to help you stay grounded in the present and understand the gifts you already have, instead of focusing on what is next.

- Spend five minutes each day with focused thoughts about the three people you care about most in the world. Often, Type 7s are so busy projecting and imagining the future, that they completely ignore others' feelings and needs. Stop this cycle.

Chapter 10

Type 8 Deep Dive

When Bryan was eight years old, his parents signed him up for basketball. This was his first real experience playing a competitive sport. It was run by the local park district and consisted of a couple of practices per week followed by games every Saturday. All the kids were divided up into teams of six players.

This might sound like the typical park district experience, but there was one big difference—the entire thing was run by one "coach"! He ran the practices, coached, and officiated the games. It is insane to think of how that man held everything together.

On game days he had each team count off one through six. He then used these numbers to make sure kids received equal playing time. It wasn't rocket science, but it was a great system. This is a system almost every youth coach has used at some point in their life.

As the games went on, he would shout out which number player had to go out of the game and which player on the bench would come in. Everyone kept playing as the players were exchanged. If this sounds atypical, that's because it was. The method much more resembled a shift change in hockey than typical basketball substitutions, but this was an outstanding system for a one-man show.

Everyone got to play, so the parents were happy and the kids had fun . . . well, most of the kids had fun.

Bryan was born with an oversized competitive streak that had stayed pretty well hidden until it reared its ugly head on a snowy Saturday morning in a small park district gym. He was in his third game of the season, and it was a real barn burner, you know, as far as eight-year-old basketball goes. To be precise, the score was 2–2, late in the second half, but, most importantly, it was time for Bryan's competitive streak to be unleashed.

Someone on the opposing team threw up a shot that missed, and the ball started bouncing toward the sideline. Bryan sprinted over and grabbed the ball before it went out of bounds. As he started dribbling down to his end of the court, the coach yelled out, "Threes!" The opposing player closest to him turned and headed for the sidelines, leaving him a clear lane to the basket. All Bryan could think about was scoring the winning basket as he was driving into the lane.

All of a sudden, the coach blew the whistle and yelled, "STOP!" right before Bryan's heroic basket.

There were too many players on the floor, and little Bryan was furious. All he could think about was which one of his teammates wasn't paying attention when "threes" were called out of the game. Since the team didn't really have a coach, he decided it was up to him to handle the "discipline."

Bryan yelled, "Who's number three?" No one answered. So, he went up to each one of his teammates, got in their faces, and barked at them, "What number are you?" With each answer, Bryan became angrier and angrier. He finally got to the last one, and knowing that it had to be him, he yelled a little louder, "What number are you?" Sheepishly, he answered, and he wasn't number three either.

Finally, it dawned on Bryan—*he* was number three. The anger quickly turned to embarrassment and shame as Bryan looked around and saw that everyone was looking at him. Needless to say, his parents had a long conversation with him on the way home from the game.

Bryan's number that day was "three," but it should have been "eight" since he was giving everyone an eyeful of what Enneagram Type 8s look like.

DESCRIPTION OF ENNEAGRAM TYPE 8
An Enneagram Type 8 is frequently called "the Challenger." They are controlling, intense, and challenging. As with all types, they have their

autopilot or default behaviors but can also exhibit a wide range of other behaviors.

Type 8s are typically charismatic and seek out opportunities to impart their will and leave their mark. This tendency can naturally lend itself to amazing accomplishments and prodigious feats that other types may never even imagine possible. These feats fueled by seemingly limitless energy and passion can inspire others to be their best or can be a fire that shines so brightly that others will self-select and choose to not follow them.

However, the downside of a Type 8's desire for intensity and control can be extremely problematic. Type 8s often find themselves walking down a path of self-destructive behaviors. In the worst cases, they tend to end up isolated and in positions in which they have alienated themselves even from those they were once closest to.

Triad

As part of the Anger Triad, Type 8s outwardly express their anger toward anyone or anything that stands in their way. The expression "not everything in life is a competition" simply does not apply to a Type 8.

If there is no competition, they will create one, and if you stand in the way of their winning or success, you become the beneficiary of the anger that drives a Type 8. For Type 8s, there are always mountains to climb and battles to be fought. This is a wonderful trait when you are standing beside a Type 8, and not so wonderful when you are standing across from them, whether it be on an athletic field, boardroom, or anything in between.

The good news is that you will never have to question what is happening with a Type 8, as they wear their emotions on their sleeves and have a far reduced fear of conflict compared to most other humans. If you have angered a Type 8, you will definitely know.

Comparison to Other Types in the Anger/Gut Triad

Anger for this triad can be compared to acid. Type 9s want to forget about or hide the acid until eventually, it builds up inside and explodes, and Type 1s hold on to the acid as it burns inside in deep resentment. Type 8s, however, want to get the acid out as soon as possible.

Motivations

Enneagram Type 8s are motivated by the need to control or exert influence over everything around them, even at the micro level. Holistically, Type 8s have a basic need to feel that they are the ones in control of their own life. Their behaviors, when on autopilot, almost always drive toward ensuring they are dictating the terms of their life. This persists even when it is counterproductive to their stated goals, or, in the case of working together, the team's goals.

Type 8s are also motivated to be strong and powerful. This concept permeates Type 8s in both the physical sense and the behavioral sense. Often, a Type 8 is not only trying to exert influence over a situation but may also be the biggest and strongest person in the room. While being intimidating is not a motivation of a Type 8, it often ends up being a default as they act on their motivations.

Fear

The basic fear of Type 8s is feeling vulnerable, feeling weak, or being controlled. Because of this fear, Type 8s lack trust in others and do not want to be at the mercy of someone else. They assume people to be untrustworthy until they have proven themselves otherwise. Type 8s provide this proving ground by challenging all who enter their realm. Push back, and you will earn the respect and trust of the Type 8. Shrink away or capitulate, and the Type 8 will run you over on the way to their goal or destination. Most people are overwhelmed by this type of behavior, and, thus, Type 8s are fiercely independent and often take on an "I'll do it myself" approach to life.

Craving

Type 8s crave intensity. It's this craving that can propel them to great things as they attempt to control the environment around them. However, this also leads them to be impulsive with an all-or-nothing approach to life, leaving them prone to overindulgence and excessive behavior. A sign of great emotional health in Type 8s is the ability to not give in to their craving for intensity and to simply not take action in every scenario. In essence, to not see the world as one mountain to climb after the other. Without this level of self-mastery, and the continued deference to their craving for intensity, Type 8s will eventually push themselves to illness, injury, and burnout.

Self-Sabotage
The motivation, fear, and craving of the Enneagram Type 8 manifest in self-sabotaging behaviors when a Type 8, operating either on autopilot or consciously, makes choices aligned with their motivations and away from their fears over their stated goals or priorities. This typically manifests itself as Type 8s seeking control instead of cooperation, and independence instead of emotionally vulnerable relationships. Ironically, this typically denies Type 8s the intensity they desire, and the cycle will start over again creating another situation in which they can exert influence. Over time, Type 8s can isolate themselves because they mistakenly choose to seek intensity through challenges and situations instead of through vulnerability and relationships.

Role on a Team
Type 8s typically ascend to leadership roles on most teams. The ascension can be natural, elected, or coerced. If there is a void in leadership or authority, the Type 8 will almost always choose to fill that void. In situations where Type 8s are not in charge, they can be a good team player as long as clear roles are defined. Usually, however, Type 8s are either in the front or the back. There is seldom an in-between.

The downside to this role is that Type 8s in the athletic realm will not always respect authority. In a recent situation, I observed a Type 8 basketball player tell an underclassman playing on the varsity basketball team to ignore his coach and not run to the corner as the play was designed and to go to the wing. This was the correct decision, leading to two open threes in a row for the underclassman . . . who was then benched for not running the play properly.

Often, the lack of respect for authority, particularly at the high school level, will not manifest in defiance toward the coach. It will result in little behaviors like the one described above, in which the player will pick and choose what to do. These decisions are almost never borne out of laziness or disregard, they are typically fueled by the desire to help reach peak performance.

Continuum of Behaviors

Every Enneagram type has default behaviors but also a predisposition to behave in different ways depending upon their emotional and behavioral

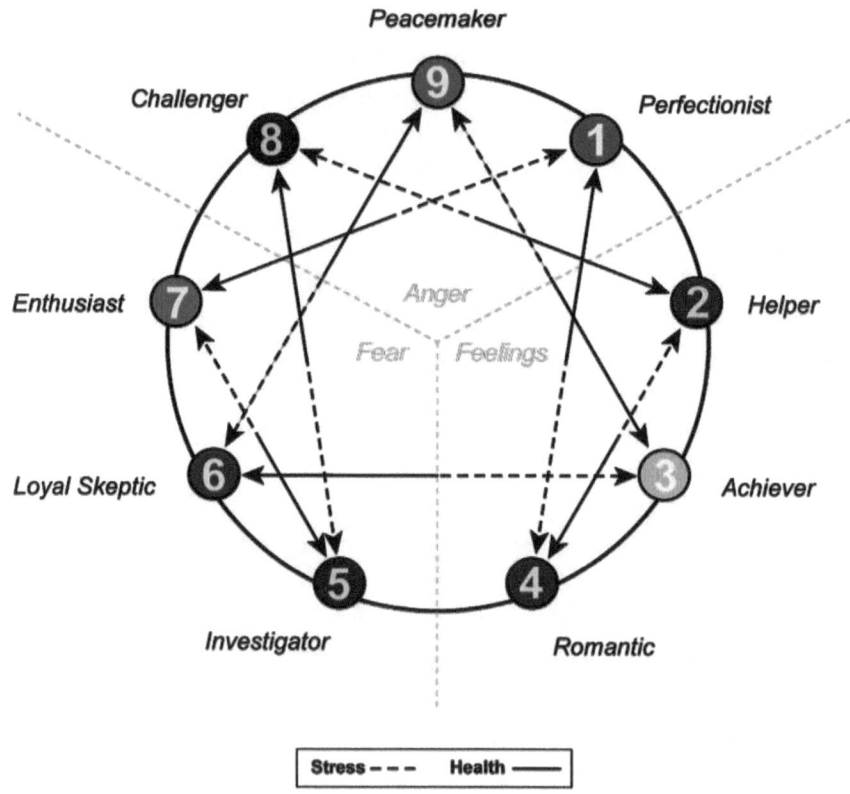

health. When healthy, Type 8s behave like Enneagram Type 2s; and when under stress, they typically behave like Enneagram Type 5s.

Healthy
Type 8s, who can be intense and controlling, become more open-hearted and empathetic, like Type 2s.

Stress
Type 8s, who are self-confident and assertive, become secretive and reclusive, like Type 5s.

Same, But Different—Enneagram Wings
Although there are nine basic personality types in the Enneagram, each type can be influenced by the types on either side, making two people of the same Enneagram type appear very different. In the case of Type 8s, they can either lean toward Type 7 or Type 9.

Type 8s with a 7-wing tend to be very charismatic, outgoing, and hard-charging. They are energized by being out in front of everyone and moving quickly from project to project. Completion isn't as important as starting. This Type 8 will push back against any perceived authority.

Type 8s with a 9-wing tend to be much more laid back and easygoing. They still want to lead and control but prefer to do it without much fanfare. Most of their hard work is unseen and is focused on one project at a time. This typically manifests in more of an all-or-nothing approach. This Type 8 will typically only push back against authority when it is in the way of them accomplishing their goals.

I might be an Enneagram 8 if . . .
- I tend to take over projects/meetings when working in a group.
- My initial reaction to anyone who challenges or questions me is anger.
- I don't trust that someone else will do their share, so I do it for them.

- My go-to reaction to mistakes during practices and games is yelling and anger.
- I push back against rules that I don't agree with but get angry when others don't follow the rules I set for them.
- I get energized by conflict or challenge.
- I create mountains to climb when there is nothing challenging me in my daily life.
- I tend to take on too much because "no one can do it like I can."
- I view rest as a manifestation of weakness.
- I sacrifice emotional engagement for accomplishing my goals.
- I suppress my emotions, so I won't appear vulnerable.

R^3

Coach Masterson was coaching a group of seventh-grade boys in an extended season round-robin basketball tournament when he unintentionally facilitated one of the biggest twelve-year-old meltdowns anyone has ever seen. This tournament was designed to give the athletes a few extra weeks of practice and game time after their season ended but before some of them began their AAU seasons and others began their track workouts. Translation—this was about as low stakes as it gets.

Throughout the course of the seventh-grade school season (which Coach Masterson did not coach), the team had won a grand total of two games. That said, he was pretty confident that he could turn this ship around. The team had a handful of practices entering the tournament, and Coach felt the team was in great shape to compete when Saturday morning arrived.

The first two games went exceptionally well, and the team defeated two teams that had handled them easily during the school season. To the shock of almost everyone, they emerged from pool play among the final four teams, and we were competing for the championship.

In the semifinals, the team found themselves down eight points in the third quarter. The team they were playing was sitting in a zone defense, and Coach only had one player whom he trusted to try to shoot their defense out of the zone. Coach Masterson called a timeout and instructed the players to run the same play until he said differently.

The team ran the same play on six straight possessions and ended up with six open shots converting on three of them. This cut their eight-point lead down to two with plenty of time left in the game. The third quarter ended and the kids came back to the huddle full of confidence and swagger thinking they were about to beat a team that had beaten them by thirty just a few weeks before.

Coach Masterson firmly announced in the huddle that he thought they were going to win and reiterated to *keep running the same play* until he told them to stop. The team took the ball to start the fourth quarter, the play worked again, and this time one of the seventh graders playing up on the team hit a three-pointer! They were up one. The crowd of twenty parents there at 1:00 p.m. on Saturday afternoon was going nuts.

For the next possession, the team they were playing switched from man to zone. Coach Masterson did not change the play, but as soon as the point guard realized that a slow-footed player from the other team wearing number eleven had switched on to him, he abandoned the play, drove to the hoop, and missed a contested layup. The next time down the court, the offense spaced the floor to start the play that had been working, and just like before, number eleven came out on the point guard again. This time, the point guard blew by his defender for an open layup.

Coach immediately called a timeout and pulled him from the game. He gave instructions to the rest of the team to continue to run the play that the point guard had abandoned, and once they left the huddle, Coach went over to the player and loudly asked why he chose not to run the play that was working.

The player shouted back that his man could not guard him and that is why we wanted them to get out of the zone in the first place. He was not wrong.

But now he was on the bench for the rest of the game for talking back. The previously mentioned twelve-year-old meltdown followed.

Coach Masterson told the point guard that he was more concerned about him learning to listen to his coach and execute plays than winning a seventh-grade off-season game. To this day, Coach remembers specifically saying to him that this situation was bigger than a layup in an empty gym. A minute went by, and Coach really wanted to check him back in the game, but he did not.

In this battle of wills, Coach Masterson lost his best player and then eventually lost the game.

Here is how the situation might have played out differently if Coach had effectively used the R^3 method and had a better understanding of himself and his players.

Review

In the moment, Coach saw a player that was not following directions and perceived he was operating in a borderline selfish manner. Coach Masterson believed that it was his responsibility to ensure that he prepared him to be successful at the next level of basketball, and he needed to be taught that listening to the coach superseded his instincts and even his successful performance.

Reset

If Coach would have taken a moment to look inward, he would have seen that, while his intentions were good, he was arbitrarily enforcing a rule created that really just gave him more control. Coach was showing the twelve-year-old who was boss. Furthermore, he knew his player well, and he should have known the exact reaction that would come from this punitive measure.

Resolve

If Coach would have taken just seconds to review and reset, he would have attempted to resolve the issue a different way. He would have put his desire for control aside and would have easily remembered that every coach at the high school level would be excited to have a player with the awareness necessary to attack a weak defender in a close game.

Moreover, if he would have taken a second to KYP (Know Your Personnel—a favorite acronym in coach speak), he would have known publicly challenging and punishing this player would have led to a meltdown. Simply letting his point guard know that as long as number eleven guarded him, he was to take advantage of the situation, but as soon as the defense changed, he needed to run the play as called, which would have led to a dramatically different outcome.

In this real-life scenario, both coach and player were Enneagram Type 8s, and as a result, both sought control and influence, losing sight of the originally intended goal of winning the game, having fun, and developing new skills. Both parties were so caught up in the moment and stuck on autopilot that they allowed their personalities to drive their behavior, ultimately leading to disappointment for both.

Tomorrow Takeaways

- Identify three areas of your life where you are asserting control in which you do not need to.
- Explore what aspects of your life would be improved if you would allow yourself to be vulnerable.
- Discuss with your team/coaches where your propensity to assert control stifles the creativity of those around you (players, coaches).
- Analyze how anger is leading you to behaviors that are counterproductive to your stated goals. Discuss this with a friend, colleague, or mentor.

Chapter 11

Type 9 Deep Dive

After a contentious Board of Education meeting in February, the decision that very few wanted to hear was confirmed. West Monroe School District and Davis Township were going to merge. This led to many difficult decisions and concessions needing to be made by members of each district. The one positive that everyone kept coming back to was that the possibility of merging both volleyball programs may just lead to an incredibly competitive team poised for a state run.

The first question to be answered was which coach would be retained and take over the program. This question was answered quickly as the more veteran coach whom everyone assumed would be awarded the position moved into the head coach role for the local community college. This left Coach Austin as the clear choice, and she was more than ready for the challenge.

The first set of obstacles that Coach Austin would have to overcome was figuring out how to turn two teams into one. She designed a set of team-building exercises and decided to give the team more authority in the planning process than usual. She believed that team-building and collaboration that had "real" implications would bring the athletes together more quickly than arbitrary challenges or rope courses.

Soon, it became clear that this transition would not be easy for anyone involved. As the group of girls moved from task to task, there were times when Coach Austin thought that she may have to physically separate them. Then, she started to notice something. Caroline Janes continued to step forward and find a way to get the group to a consensus.

Chapter 11

Caroline's behavior persisted through all of the challenges and through the off-season workouts. She was the one who finally was able to get the two text threads to merge, and was even able to successfully navigate the process of determining how the warm-up music for each game would be selected.

As you might imagine, Coach Austin was not particularly concerned with the warm-up music. That said, she was somewhat amazed watching Caroline navigate the decision-making process. Ultimately, the team decided to come out to a mix of country and techno, and, somehow, everyone seemed happy. Once the decision was made, Coach asked Caroline about the decision. She laughed and said she hated both and loved hard rock from "back in the day—probably when you were in school, Coach."

Coach Austin was taken aback. Not by the comment implicating her advanced age—she actually thought that was hilarious—but she was amazed that Caroline put her needs and wants far behind what was best for the team to reach a consensus. Not only did she do that but also she led the process that led to that decision.

When off-season workouts ended, Coach Austin asked the team to select their captain. This was a truly democratic process and one that Coach Austin was not involved in outside of insisting that the program selected a captain at each level of competition. The votes came in quickly, and Caroline was almost a unanimous decision to be Varsity Captain.

This was surprising for two reasons. First, Caroline was a junior. Second, she was not projected to get very much playing time. Caroline was a fine player but not a standout. To be clear, she was not going to start, but she may have if the consolidation did not occur. Still, the athletes had spoken—she was their leader.

The season was difficult off the court. The team was still coming together, and there were distinct factions among the athletes. Time after time, Caroline came to the rescue. She solved a multitude of crises that Coach Austin knew about, plus about three times as many that never made it out of the locker room.

The good news was that all of this difficult work was allowing a great season to take place on the court. The team started to achieve all of the goals that they set. First, it was a conference championship, then a regional championship, then a sectional championship, and, finally, they made it all the way to state. They lost in the Final Four, but the team was young and the future was bright. More importantly, the success on the court and the time together started to bring the team together as one.

At the conclusion of the season, Coach Austin announced that she was naming Caroline captain for her senior year. The girls in the locker room gave her a standing ovation in unanimous support. They realized all that she had done to keep the season progressing forward.

During the off-season, Coach Austin met often with Caroline to outline the expectations she had for a captain during a more typical season. She discussed the decision-making authority she would have and the expectation for her to lead Friday practices. She also explained that on her highly successful collegiate team, the first line of discipline for violation of team rules came from the captain.

Throughout these conversations, Caroline nodded and did not push back. As the season approached, Caroline started to share some inklings that she was not comfortable with the responsibilities given to her. Coach would respond with one of her favorite sayings, "On bad teams, nobody leads. On good teams, coaches lead. On great teams, players lead." She would then remind Caroline that this team had a chance to be a great team. Caroline acquiesced, and the season started.

Everything and everyone seemed to struggle. Caroline was forced to move from mediator and problem-solver to someone who was setting expectations and driving accountability. She was not strong at doing either of those things, and she *hated* doing both. Moreover, she lost her role as peacemaker on the team because she was too busy trying to perform other "leadership" duties.

Coach Austin saw this happening in slow motion. She watched the off-season become less and less productive as the weeks moved forward. She brought Caroline in and diagnosed the problem. She had taken all of her natural strengths away and asked her to be someone she wasn't. Coach asked if it was okay with her if she named a co-captain that could balance her strengths and mitigate her areas of potential growth. Caroline was ecstatic.

The season was saved. It was saved because Coach Austin had the humility to mid-course correct and the understanding of personality archetypes to discern that she placed Caroline in a position that did not support her innate personality traits and gifts. This judgment saved the season and put Caroline (and her team) in a position to succeed.

Description of Enneagram Type 9

An Enneagram Type 9 is also known as "the Peacemaker." Peacemakers, as the name implies, are focused on maintaining the status quo of both the groups they are a part of, as well as their own personal normal. Type 9s do not want to rock the boat, and are commonly perceived as pleasant, laid-back, and accommodating. Type 9s prefer to go along with the thoughts, ideas, and behaviors of others.

The behaviors of Type 9s are all driven by the motivation to avoid conflict of any kind. This manifests itself in the Type 9's desire to blend in and become part of the crowd. Because of this desire to keep the peace, Type 9s, when healthy, have the unique ability to see both sides of an issue. This positions them to be terrific leaders, negotiators, and mediators.

At their worst, Type 9s' desire to avoid conflict can push them to ignore their own ideas and desires, preferring to merge with others and seek consensus at all times. Robbed of their drive for life, Type 9s can slow down to a crawl and become dependent on others for direction, not wanting to make waves.

Triad

As part of the Anger Triad, Type 9s suppress their anger to maintain an illusion of peace, both in their inner and outer worlds. This suppression can last only so long and has to be released in one of two ways. The first is in a short-lived outburst, and the second is through consistent passive-aggressive behavior.

Unfortunately, for some unsuspecting bystanders, this short outburst relief valve for a Type 9's anger is often released in an explosion at some benign or inopportune time. Unlike some other Enneagram types, as quickly as it comes for a Type 9, the anger is shoved back down. However, this anger will only continue to build up for the next unlucky victim.

The other way their anger manifests is in biting passive-aggressiveness. As Type 9s become attached to this good-guy or good-girl persona, resentment and anger builds as they continually sacrifice their own wishes and ideas for the "good" of the group. This frustration can be expressed as stubbornness, avoidance, procrastination, or the silent treatment as resentment builds. Type 9s work hard, however, to make the microaggressions small enough in nature to not disrupt the status quo of the group but large enough to be noticeable to someone who is not overtly looking for such behavior.

Comparison to Other Types in the Anger/Gut Triad
Anger for this triad can be compared to acid. Type 8s want to get the acid out as soon as possible, and Type 1s hold on to the acid as it burns inside as deep seething resentment. However, Type 9s try to forget about or hide the acid until eventually, it builds up inside and explodes.

Motivations
Enneagram Type 9s are motivated by the need to avoid conflict at all costs. Type 9s believe that in order to be loved and of value to others, they have to go along with the crowd. The goal of the Type 9 is to blend in and sit in the background, as if to take on the moniker "If I become invisible and forget my wants and needs, I can eliminate any confrontation or conflict from my life."

As such, Type 9s shrink away from challenges and, sadly, their own dreams. This motivation leads to the avoidance of expending energy toward anything in life that may make waves with others. Type 9s have the least amount of energy of all the Enneagram types, preferring to stay in a sloth-like state and hoping everything continues to go smoothly. This low-energy state is very hard to break free from and can often give Type 9s the appearance of being lazy.

Fear

The basic fear of the Type 9 is that of loss or separation from the group. It is this fear that really drives their almost pathological conflict avoidance. They believe that if they can ignore their impulses and forget their desires, they can remain in the group and no one will leave them.

Psychologically, this behavioral tendency usually stems from feeling overlooked or perceived as being less important as children. With this fear left unchecked and operating on default, the Type 9s suppression of their innate drive and ambition leaves them dependent on others for any advancement in life. At times, it seems as though a Type 9 must be pushed along against their will to move anywhere for fear of losing connection to their happy place. No Enneagram type benefits more from surrounding themselves with a successful group of people, nor will any Enneagram type outside of Type 9 be more negatively impacted by associating with the wrong type of people.

Craving

Type 9s want peace and harmony. This single-minded focus on keeping the peace and avoiding confrontation shapes their behaviors. Additionally, they love routine—they will drive the same route to work every day, wake up at the same time every day, eat the same food every day, and even have a specific "uniform" they will wear for each day of the week.

Type 9s will stay in the same job, even if it is one they don't like, or stay in a relationship that brings them no joy because being part of something toxic is better than being alone. As a leader or coach, getting a Type 9 to change any of these routines is a Herculean effort. Type 9s live life by the rule, "If it ain't broke, don't fix it." Their stubbornness is born directly from their craving for peace and harmony.

However, this craving can also be a source of strength for Type 9s. The innate comfort a Type 9 has with routines lends itself to Type 9s being process-driven. The longer and more regular the process, the more Type 9s will dig into it. Type 9s thrive when the process, instead of the outcome, can be the winner. They will manage and facilitate processes fanatically, and, in time, Type 9s can lead incredible incremental change.

Self-Sabotage

The motivation, fear, and craving of the Enneagram Type 9 manifest in self-sabotaging behavior when a Type 9 is operating on autopilot and does not realize they are trapped in their circle of sameness. Being completely unaware that they are riding the same hamster wheel day after day, Type 9s fall in love with knowing what's around every corner.

Whether consciously or unconsciously, the longer they stay in this "Groundhog Day," the more entrapped they become and the more resistant they will become to anyone trying to disrupt their status quo—including themselves. Stubbornly unwilling to move on to a different path, the months and years roll by with little to no change for the Type 9. As others change and grow, moving to different places and levels in life, Type 9s must face a choice: stay on autopilot and face a life lived to make other people comfortable and content, or allow themselves to be led to a different place, becoming dependent on the one they are following.

Role on a Team

Type 9s can occupy any number of roles on a team. The average Type 9 will be content to blend in with the team, almost becoming an invisible member if allowed. A Type 9 is the prototypical "worker bee." They will quietly focus on doing the job that was assigned to them, hoping not to stand out too much, positively or negatively.

Healthy and aware Type 9s, however, can ascend to become strong, collaborative, and popular leaders. The unique abilities to see both sides of an issue, mediate, and avoid conflict allow Type 9s to unite a team in a way that other types cannot.

Unfortunately, a prototypical Type 9 can work in the same position for years unnoticed. That said, successful Type 9s can play an intricate role in helping a team be successful. Behind the scenes, the Type 9 may be acting as a great buffer between a hard-nosed coach and their players by playing the role of "good cop."

Additionally, a Type 9 can act as a great insulator, keeping small problems from becoming big so that the leader of the program can focus on other more important tasks. This is not to say a Type 9 cannot be

Chapter 11

a great coach on their own. At their peak, a Type 9 can certainly be a beloved head coach that creates a family-like program.

Continuum of Behaviors

Every Enneagram type has default behaviors but also a predisposition to behave in different ways depending upon their emotional and behavioral health. When healthy, Type 9s behave like Enneagram Type 3s; and when under stress, they typically behave like Enneagram Type 6s.

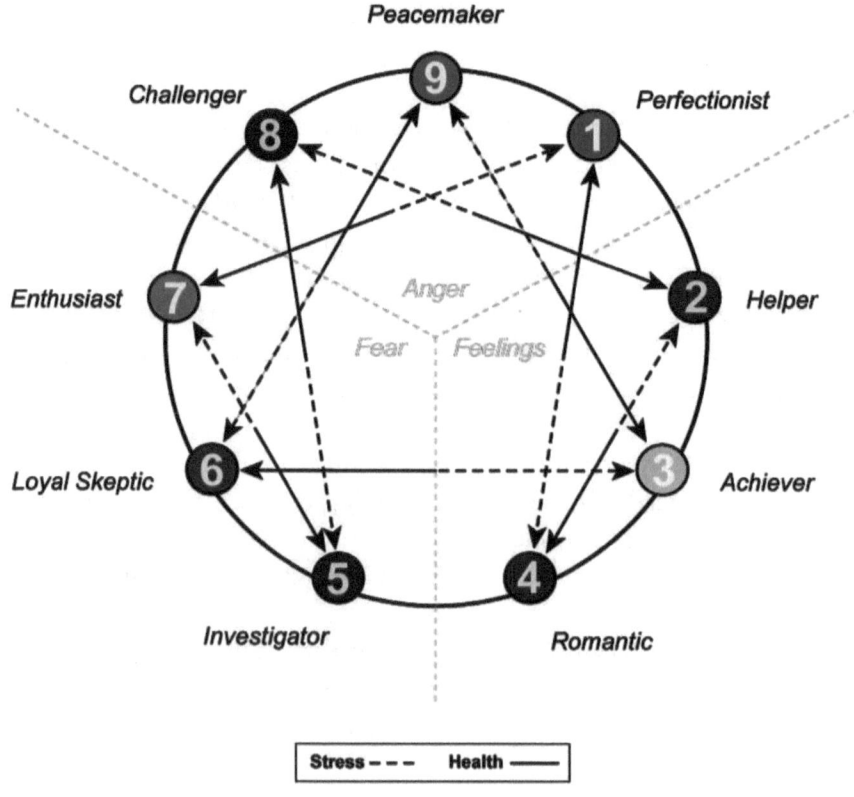

Healthy

Type 9s, who can be lazy and complacent, become more energetic and goal-oriented, like Type 3s.

Stress

Type 9s, who are laid-back and easygoing, become anxious and overcommitted, like Type 6s.

Same, But Different—Enneagram Wings

Although there are nine basic personality types in the Enneagram, each type can be influenced by the types on either side, making two people of the same Enneagram type appear very different. In the case of Type 9s, they can either lean toward Type 8 or Type 1.

Type 9s with an 8-wing tend to be more confident, inner-directed, and outgoing than your average Type 9. They are much more expressive with their anger but are quick to de-escalate the situation. This type of 9 is a great advocate for the underdog and the common good.

Type 9s with a 1-wing tend to be more critical, orderly, and passive-aggressive. They have a strong sense of right and wrong, and look at the work they do as more black and white. As a result of the increased focus brought over by the 1-wing, they have the energy to stay on task and accomplish more goals than the prototypical Type 9.

I might be an Enneagram Type 9 if...

- I avoid conflict at all costs.
- I am very comfortable with routine. If I had my way, every day would be the same.
- I tend to choose the path of least resistance, even if it takes me away from my goals.
- I have a gift of being able to see all sides of an issue.
- If people put too many expectations on me, I will shut down and tune them out.

- I have a hard time saying no, and this may lead me to grow resentful of those asking me to do things over and over again.
- I tend to procrastinate. I have never been accused of being a self-starter.
- I have a hard time being decisive. I would much rather just stay where I am.
- I rarely speak up if I have an opinion or an idea. Rather, I will just go along with what others think.
- I often find myself being a referee with my family and my friends.

R^3

On the first day of football camp for Steven Bryant in his junior year at Limewire College, he met the most gifted athlete he had ever been around. Immediately upon walking on the practice field, it was clear that this freshman was different, and Steven could not wait to see where his addition to the team would take the season.

The freshman's name was Tom Wheeler. Everyone called him Tommy. Tommy, as is the case with all freshmen, had no clue where things went or what was expected of him. His locker was right next to Steven, and being a team captain, at the first opportunity presented, Steven introduced himself. As Steven stuck out his hand for a hardy "Welcome to the Team" handshake, he couldn't help but notice the enormity of Tommy's hand. Steven was a fairly decent-sized guy, but his hand looked like a child's compared to Tommy's and his grip was just as impressive!

Tommy was a well-sculpted 235 pounds on a 6'5" frame. He could run like the wind and jump out of the gym. As they began all of the testing and drills at the start of camp, it was obvious that, even though he was a freshman, he was the best athlete on the field. He dominated every drill, every lift, and every scrimmage. He quickly ascended to the top of the depth chart at tight end.

As the season began, one thing about Tommy became clear—he was probably the nicest human being you would ever meet. With all his talent and success, he had every opportunity to be the loud, cocky freshman that is stereotypical of any college sports movie, but that wasn't Tommy. He was reserved, and while he was not shy, he was definitely not outgoing.

Socially, he was never going to be the life of the party, but he'd definitely be there having a good time. Steven always admired that Tommy had a constant smile on his face. He had one of those smiles that just seemed to put everyone at ease, and it was rare that he was ever seen without it.

With all of his athletic ability and his easygoing personality, it never seemed like Tommy was trying that hard. Everything looked as though it was just smooth and easy. It would look like he was just jogging as he blew past someone on a go-route. The coaches would simply have to point him in the right direction, and tell him which technique to use, and he would do it with ease and make it work.

He was an easy teammate to have and an easy player for Steven to mentor. He was always on time and got everything done that needed to be done. Everything was running as smoothly as possible for the first couple of weeks of the regular season. It wasn't until the homecoming game against their biggest rival that things took a turn.

Coach Parsons was the longtime coach at Limewire. Coach was a pretty fiery individual. He wasn't yelling and screaming all day long, but he definitely got after the players when he needed to. Most players respected Coach Parsons for treating everyone the same way. There was absolutely no favoritism from Coach, and it didn't matter if you were team captain or third-string punter, no one was immune from a good butt-chewing once in a while. Additionally, playing time was earned every day. Nobody could rest on their reputation or on what they did in the past at Limewire.

Late in the second quarter of the homecoming game, it was a tie game. Limewire was driving and looking to punch one in to take the lead. Limewire was solid but was not expected to hang close in this game. That made this drive even more important. Coach believed that being up a score at halftime would be a huge lift.

Coach sent in a pass play that was designed to go to Tommy. When the quarterback called the play in the huddle, everyone looked at each other and smiled. Tommy had been killing them the whole game. No one on the other team could cover him. All he had to do was get in the end zone so the quarterback could throw it up to him.

The play gave Tommy freedom. He had to read the defense and break in or out depending on what alignment the defense was in. This play design required a ton of trust. Both the quarterback and receiver have to interpret the defense in the same manner in real time and make the same split-second decision.

The play was so complex in that regard that Steven was even surprised. Limewire had long practiced this play but had never run it during a game in his two-plus years in the program. That said, with Tommy's athleticism, no one really gave it a thought. Just throw it up, and go get it for a touchdown.

Unfortunately, Tommy made the wrong choice. The quarterback threw the out, and Tommy ran inside. You could almost see the quarterback trying to pull the ball back to his hand after he let it go. He threw a perfect ball. Just to the wrong team. Tommy turned to look for the ball, just as the defender caught it and was headed the other way. Just like that—there was a fourteen-point swing. There is nothing more deflating than going from seven up to down seven in a matter of seconds.

Head down, Tommy jogged off to the sidelines, where an irate Coach Parsons was waiting. The Limewire upperclassmen all knew he was going to get the chewing of a lifetime. He stood there and took it, then sat slumped on the bench as the time in the half ran out.

If that would have been the end of it, Tommy probably would have been just fine. But the coach continued his tirade in the locker room at halftime, into the second half, and through the rest of the season.

Suddenly, the effortless ease that Tommy moved and played with was perceived by Coach as not trying hard. His easygoing attitude was now perceived as being lazy. Coach's answer was simply to yell more to "motivate" him, and the assistant coaches followed suit. The more they pushed and yelled, the more Tommy withdrew. His ever-present smile was replaced with an indifferent look. He started showing up late to practice and meetings, further enraging the coaching staff, and perpetuating the myth about his work ethic.

For all the promise at the beginning of the season, Tommy was an afterthought by the end. Needless to say that this was his one and only season playing football.

Here is how Limewire's season might have been saved had Coach Parsons used the R^3 method and had a better understanding of Enneagram.

Review

If Coach Parsons would have known about the Enneagram and taken a step back from the situation, he would have seen that Tommy was an Enneagram Type 9. His default was set to easygoing. He wanted to avoid conflict at all costs.

Coach Parsons yelling at him and putting more and more expectations on him only made Tommy retreat further into himself and become angrier at the situation. Since conflict avoidance is the hallmark of all Type 9s, this anger manifested itself in the passive-aggressive behaviors of showing up late to meetings and practice.

Reset

In this scenario, the fatal flaw in the coach's "one size fits all" approach to dealing with his players was exposed. Tommy didn't need to be screamed at for more motivation. What he needed was an explanation of what he did wrong, how to avoid making the same mistake again, and a pat on the back saying we'll get them next time.

Type 9s, probably more than any other type, do not respond well to pressure or stress. Moreover, expecting a surge of energy or perceived effort as a result of holding Type 9s accountable, particularly in public, is simply not going to happen. In order to change their behavior, coaches or leaders should attempt to match their calm demeanor and limit the amount of independent and consequential decisions they need to make. Doing so is the key to maximizing their potential.

Resolve

Once the coach realized what Enneagram type Tommy was, he would have changed the approach he and his assistants used. Instead of constantly challenging, yelling, and even demeaning him, they should have used encouragement and rewarded the behavior they wanted out of Tommy. When everything was going well at the beginning of the season, there was no pressure on Tommy and he could just be himself. With those conditions, he was a dominating presence and a major asset to the team.

Type 9s are fantastic teammates and leaders when they are moving to the healthy side of their personality. They have an uncanny knack for bringing people together and smoothing over disagreements. Type 9s perform best when fitted to established processes and routines.

Their true nature of not wanting to rock the boat robs their decision-making processes and inhibits many self-directed behaviors. The most common mistake when leading or coaching a Type 9 is to think that they can be "forced" into the behavior or role.

Thinking that you can will, direct, or demean a Type 9 to behave in the manner you so choose leads two things to happen. First, the Type 9 will shut down and tune out. This is the best possible outcome in this situation. Often, this just leads to a master class in passive-aggressiveness from the Type 9. Second, frustration builds from the coach or leader who tries harder and harder to motivate the "lazy" Type 9 to either change their behavior or perform at a higher level. This ultimately will lead to the Type 9 exploding out of anger or choosing to remove themselves from the situation altogether.

Tomorrow Takeaways

- Analyze how often you don't speak up and share your opinion or ideas during a meeting or conversation. How many times has that cost your team or yourself an opportunity? How many times has it made a situation worse?
- Ask yourself what your life's purpose is. If that is too big of a question, analyze what you can contribute to your team or a relationship. Create some action steps to move you in this direction.
- Analyze how you shut down when too much is asked of you. What passive-aggressive behaviors do you implement?

Procrastination? Avoidance? How have these behaviors made situations worse by having even more pressure and expectations put on you?

- Evaluate your peer group and determine whether their ambition and trajectory are impacting yours—positively or negatively.
- Staying focused on a project or what needs to be done is a weaker area for you. So find the best way to keep yourself on task. Make a list and find the best resource to hold yourself accountable, whether that is a coach, app, or some other technique.
- Remember that objects in motion tend to stay in motion. Start and stick to an exercise program to fight the inertia of slowing down to a crawl.

Chapter 12

Self-Awareness

"You can't leave a place you've never been." –Nathaniel Brandon

The Three Ingredients to Success

There are three ingredients to success. The first is awareness. As stated previously, it is the single most important thing a person needs for success. Nothing you learn, whether it be a new offensive philosophy, defensive scheme, time-management tool, or training program, will matter if you don't start with self-awareness and parlay that into deepening your understanding of your team, creating precise situational awareness. Anything different you try will be met unconsciously with the same old habits you have developed over a lifetime.

The second is decisiveness. All successful people are decisive. It is the ability to make clear, well-informed, and timely decisions. They look at the options before them, quickly make a choice, and stick with it. What separates decisive people from other people is the speed at which they make a decision and the conviction with which they move forward with it. As the situation changes or they realize they made a wrong decision, they quickly change course and move forward again. They repeat this pattern so quickly that it may appear that they are always making the right choice, but in reality, they are simply able to adapt and choose a different path rapidly because they are decisive.

The third ingredient is the ability to take action. "Done is better than perfect!" Nothing in your life will ever change if you don't take action. Life is not a static entity. It is constantly changing. Opportunities will pop up and disappear in the blink of an eye. Waiting on the sidelines for them to show up again is a recipe for disaster.

Life bends itself to those who take action. How many times have you been coaching or watching a game where one team is just dominating another, but then, all of a sudden, one thing completely changes the momentum? A hustle play that leads to a fumble recovery, or wrestling for a loose ball, or someone sacrificing their body to block a shot on goal. Now the team that was dominating (taking action) begins to get passive. They begin to play "not to lose" instead of to win. The other team becomes assertive, takes action, and comes back for the win. This is just as true in life as it is in sports.

Part Three of this book is simply our call to action. Throughout this book, we have provided tools for you to work on yourself, and now in this chapter, we provide some additional step-by-step instructions on how to increase your awareness. The bottom line is that now that you have these tools, it is time to make a decision and take action.

Not only do you have the tools necessary to do so but also you should see the connection between these three steps to success and the process we have preached throughout the book: Review – Reset – Resolve.

These ingredients are the driving force behind our three-step process of Review - Reset - Resolve. In order to "Review" the outcomes of situations, circumstances, and events in your life, you have to have a keen sense of awareness. To "Reset" your behavior and improve these outcomes, you have to be decisive and choose a different path or response. To "Resolve" that this new behavior will be the one you will use moving forward, you have to take action. Saying you are going to change is not the same as actually changing.

Every time the process iterates, it immediately starts back over. This is the beauty of cracking the coaching code and moving forward with self-awareness. If you commit to this, you will always be improving, but never done. This becomes *you* versus *you*—the paradox that drives us all. Then the process starts all over again with you being self-aware enough

SELF-AWARENESS

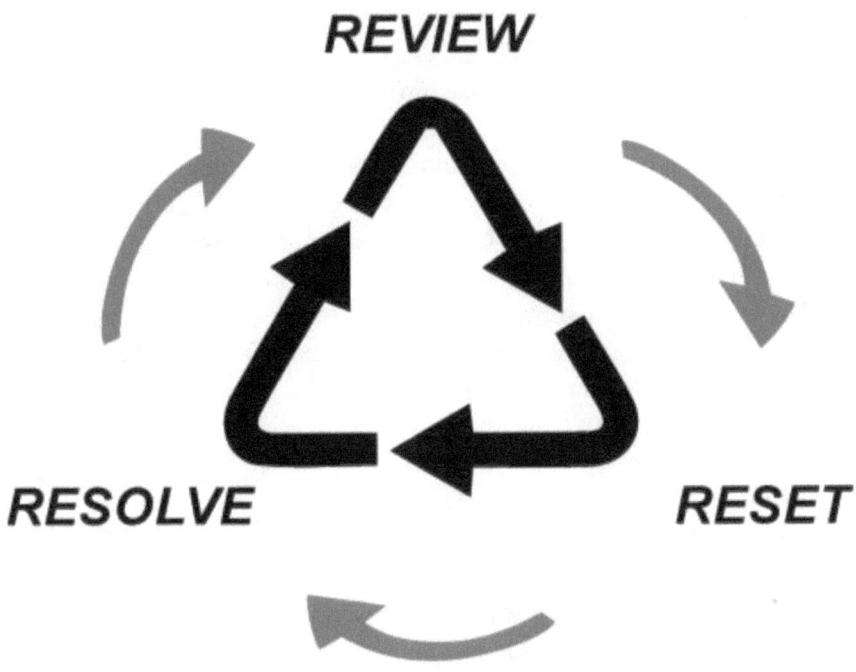

to recognize if you are sticking to the new behavior/response, or if you are falling back into the same old patterns.

> *"Make sure your worst enemy doesn't live between your own two ears."* –Laird Hamilton

A few years ago, a conversation was taking place between an athletic director and their leadership coach. The coaching relationship was borne out of friendship, and the athletic director, Matt, was always open and communicative, making the coaching process productive, but certainly not easy.

During this coaching session, Matt was venting his frustrations over a coach he recently hired. Matt went on and on about the new coach and how his x's and o's were subpar, he lacked any sort of confrontational skills with both parents and kids, and his energy level was just flat. However, the most maddening thing was that he had a tremendous amount of untapped potential.

From the sounds of it, this coach was struggling with every aspect of being a head coach.

While this situation may sound dire, having coached Matt for a few years, Phil knew this to have become a common refrain. As a coach, this did not make the situation any less important, but this was not a situation that was in any way surprising.

The conversation continued, Phil could feel the anger building in Matt's voice the more he spoke about this particular coach. We have all been in a situation where we, quite literally, talked ourselves into being angrier. That was precisely what Matt was doing.

So, Phil re-focused the conversation and asked a probing question that assigned ownership back to Matt.

Phil asked Matt what his plan was to grow this coach into the leader he could be.

An immediate response was fired back, and it was a predictable one.

He said, "I'm going to ride him until he either gets better or quits."

This was predictable because of Matt's past actions. In using Enneagram to support the coaching process, it was clear that Matt was a Type 8. Moreover, Matt was your prototypical Type 8, who, despite efforts to increase his awareness, often resorted back to his autopilot behaviors between our coaching sessions.

Phil decided to push Matt a little further. "This is coach number three in five years for this position, correct?" Matt replied, "Yes."

So Matt was forced to ponder, "Is it harder being a coach in your district?"

"I don't think so. I'd like to think we hold our staff to a higher standard, but I wouldn't say it is harder." Matt said.

The facts were clear. No other leader had burned through three coaches in five years. Not only did other schools in the area not operate like that but many also hired the coaches Matt had discarded, and some of those same coaches were enjoying more success than the same programs at Matt's school.

When challenged with these facts and asked why he thought that was, Matt's silence was deafening. You could see that despite receiving coaching, he'd never looked hard enough internally to consider that question, and was struggling to find an answer.

Phil brought him back to the Enneagram principles and teachings introduced to him a couple of years earlier and began to push forward.

"What Enneagram type is this coach?"

"He's a Type 9," he said.

"So if you 'ride' him, what will most likely be his response?"

"He'll probably shut down."

At this point in the dialogue, Phil decided that when coaching a Type 8, sometimes direct is the language they will understand best. So, he let this fly: "And you'll be hiring a fourth coach in six years."

This was the lightbulb moment for Matt. This was the moment that he transitioned from blaming others for his situation and always looking outward, to taking a deep look inward.

Unfortunately for Matt, he had fallen prey to a behavior that we all have succumbed to at one time or another—living life on autopilot. To live on autopilot or by default means to surrender our behaviors to the preprogrammed responses and habits created in our brains.

This does not have to be the case. We have the unique ability to understand what the default reaction or response might be and choose another one that will get us closer to our ultimate goal. Matt lost this sense of ownership and focus when it came to dealing with personnel issues.

Every time he was confronted with a personnel issue, or someone that wasn't living up to his standards, he responded exactly the same—he "rode" them until they improved or quit. There was no thinking or thought process, just autopilot. This behavior was so ingrained in his personality that he didn't even realize it was his automatic response and one that he had been using for years. The result would always be the same. He would run off anyone who could not withstand his pressure and then would blame them for not being stronger and able to withstand his "leadership."

Chapter 12

Why We Move to Default

Our brains have an incredible capacity to take in, process, and integrate a tremendous amount of data. However, all of this comes at a heavy cost in terms of energy. If you do not immediately believe this, think about the exhaustion you can feel after learning something new while sitting sedentary in a classroom. Our brains require an immense amount of energy. Specifically, while our brains are typically around 2 percent of our mass, they require 20 percent of the energy our body spends.

Thus, in order to conserve energy and to allow us to respond to our environments quickly, our brains create powerful circuits in our basal ganglia called habits. Habits allow us to skip the "thinking" required to respond to repeated stimuli. An example of this is at a stoplight. When you see a red light, you don't have to think about taking your foot off the accelerator and depressing the brake to stop the car. The habit you have created from years of performing this task will take over so your brain is free to focus on other tasks.

I always imagine the learning process and the habit-forming process like going on a hike through tall grass. The first few times you hike the path, it will take significantly more energy to traverse the high grass. After many, say thirty, hikes, the grass is trampled and the hike becomes much easier and requires less energy. This is akin to how connections between our synapses happen in our brain and why the brain typically chooses to use the more well-traveled path.

Our brains have created habits for every repeated stimulus in our lives. Unfortunately for us, our brains have become so adept at creating habits, we can walk around in our daily lives without putting thought into anything we are doing. Our goal is to help you realize your power in this process and to help increase your awareness.

For example, consider these questions. How many times throughout the day do you really stop and think about what you are doing or how you are responding to an event or a question? You pass someone in the hall or on the street, what do you reflexively ask? "Hi. How are you doing today?" (Or some variation of that question.) You don't even think about it. You're on autopilot. You have learned this behavior through observation and have repeated it so many times it is just a habit now.

Now, here's the crazy part: What does the other person say back to you? "Fine. How are you?" (Or, again, some variation of this.) They don't even hear the question that you asked.

If you do not think we are stuck on autopilot to the extreme we are showing here, try this no-risk, no-cost social experiment.

The next time you address someone, especially in passing, ask a different question. "Hi. What have you been doing today?" Without fail, you'll get their preprogrammed response, "Fine. How are you?" They can't help it. The habit skips over the prefrontal cortex, the portion of the brain that controls cognitive function and response flexibility, and jumps straight to the habit that has been created.

If you want to have a laugh, start asking different questions when you meet people. "Hi. where are you headed?" "Fine. How are you?" "Hi. I love your shoes." "Fine. How are you?" If you look at them quizzically or ask them what they said, it will stop them in their tracks.

Organizationally, we play this game with our clients. The result is usually getting a good laugh once people realize what they did and a valuable opening to show them how they are currently stuck on autopilot.

The Good News

Fortunately for us, habits can be broken. The problem is that we must first become aware that we even have these habits. When these habits are rooted in or serve to limit our self-awareness, acknowledging these habits requires a willingness to be vulnerable.

The gift on the other side of this internal evaluation and vulnerability is self-awareness. Self-awareness is the most important skill one can have to be successful in any endeavor in life.

Without self-awareness, it is exponentially more difficult to grow or succeed. Without self-awareness, we are trapped in our self-made prison of habits that continually give us the same outcomes.

If right now you are trying to figure out whether or not you have a high level of self-awareness, please consider these questions:

- Do you ever feel like no matter what you do, life keeps throwing up the same roadblocks to your success?

- Does it often feel like bad luck just seems to follow you around?
- Are you frustrated that despite significant effort you just can't seem to break through to that next level of success or achievement?

While there are many more questions we could pose, if you strongly identify with any or all of those questions, chances are you are stuck on autopilot. Said more pointedly—you are the reason the roadblocks are appearing, growth has stagnated, and the luck around you seems to be bad. This is a result of all of your habits, your pre-programmed responses, and your muscle memory keeping you firmly planted where you are.

Self-awareness is the key to ascending past this invisible ceiling you have placed on your potential. Once you are actively engaged in deepening your self-awareness, you will feel freedom to achieve all the success and happiness you desire.

However, self-awareness is very difficult to attain all on your own. You need the right tools and strategies to guide you on this journey. The Enneagram is the perfect tool for self-discovery, but most people need support to unlock its true potential.

Enneagram will point out all of the shortcomings and superpowers of our personality, and it gives us a blueprint of how to move from our average stagnate selves to the best version of us. This is a massive advantage in unlocking your self-awareness, but it still requires work.

Enneagram is like having your opponent's scouting report on you. The tool will report succinctly and clearly on all of your strengths, all of your weaknesses, and most importantly, all of your behavioral tendencies.

The tool, like this book, is designed for you to study, learn, and grow from. The only things required of you to start creating the change you wish to see are the willingness to be vulnerable and honest with yourself, and your commitment to change.

FIVE ACTIVITIES YOU CAN BEGIN IMMEDIATELY TO INCREASE YOUR SELF-AWARENESS

Self-awareness is a skill that takes a great deal of effort and persistence to master without the right tools and strategies. This entire book has been

Self-Awareness

about Enneagram, so obviously, it is our suggested tool for increasing self-awareness. That said, here is a play-by-play of how we suggest you move forward from here or help someone move forward in their journey if they are not going to read this book.

What follows are five core strategies to foster your own self-awareness:

1. Take an RHETI test to get an idea of what type you are.

   From reading this book and investigating each Enneagram type, you may have a level of confidence that you have already figured out which type you are. It always helps to reaffirm these conclusions because people frequently get this wrong. There is no shortage of free RHETI tests online that can be found with a quick Google search.

   Many times, when people take a free, online assessment they will end up with multiple Enneagram types with similar scores. This frequently leads to confusion over which type you really are. While we will provide additional strategies below, one tried and true strategy is to have a loved one take the assessment for you by answering with your common behaviors. This typically helps to provide immediate clarity.

   Once you have identified your Enneagram type, the two immediate questions and areas of focus for your study should be:

   - To ask yourself what motivates you and what your fears are.
   - To evaluate how you act when you are under stress or angry.
     Use the tools provided in this book and through the various other free online resources surrounding Enneagram to begin to learn about your default reactions. Once you have a strong gauge of where you are when you are on autopilot, you are taking the first steps in the self-awareness journey.

2. Journal.

   If a coach is committed to increasing their self-awareness, then each practice or game should end with some structured self-reflection. Reflection is an absolutely necessary tool if you are seeking to increase your self-awareness. However, if you simply play the day back in your head like a movie, reflection becomes a limited strategy.

Reflection in order to crack the coaching code should focus on deeper questions and probes that help you see yourself and those you have the privilege of leading in a different manner than your default. The following questions are recommended to use as prompts for your journaling:

- What events/conditions/interactions/situations caused me to lose emotional control?
- What was driving me to lose this control? My anger? My fear that I wasn't doing something right? The image I have of what a coach should look like?
- At what points today was I acting on autopilot? How did this hinder/help me prepare my team for success?
- How often did I consider how the person I was coaching would react based on what I knew about them, instead of behaving by default?
- In what situations do I continue to get the same results that frustrate me, and what am I actively doing to procure different results?

3. Create a 360-degree perspective.

In many management and leadership roles, a 360-degree evaluation process is used. This is where self-assessment and evaluation by your superiors, peers, and subordinates are all combined to gain a deeper understanding of your performance as it is viewed holistically.

There is no need, however, to wait for a formal evaluation process to procure this information. The following protocol will absolutely increase self-awareness and enhance relationships when those around you learn you are truly committed to your own growth. Here is the quick and easy how-to:

- Interview five people that are closest to you.
- Ask them what their perceptions of you are.

- Are you cool under pressure?
- Are you quick to anger?
- Are you low energy?
- Do you make decisions easily?
- Are you adaptable?

- Compare and analyze their responses based on what roles they know you in. For instance, if your assistant coach and a player describe a completely different person than your spouse and boss that should be informative.
- Use the information procured to compare and contrast to what you learned in steps one and two provided in this chapter.

4. Hire a coach or mentor.

No matter what your level of self-awareness, or your desire to grow your self-awareness, we all have blind spots. Using a real-world example, one of the best executive and leadership coaches in our profession frequently talks about how she employs two coaches for herself. Intuitively, you may ask why someone who is so adept at helping people look inward needs support for herself. The answer is simple; we all need support from time to time. Our default behaviors and whom we become under stress are not things that we fix, they are aspects that we must continually address.

Coaches can help you confirm your self-analysis and show you a way to break free from your bad habits. This process is iterative and emerging. You are not the same person you were five years ago, and even with increased self-awareness, the person you are in six months will need support to be the person you desire to be in twenty-four months.

Quick disclaimer—coaches and mentors are best found outside of your organization. As a supervisor, as much as the desire may be to invest in someone altruistically, by default there is also concern with the results they produce. As a coach or mentor outside of the organization, one has the ability to focus solely on the individual and their growth.

5. Video confirmation.

Nothing will more dramatically increase your level of self-awareness than an intensive video session analyzing only you during practice and games. Video can help you see and recognize consistently repeated behaviors and whether these behaviors help or hurt your ability to improve your players' performance.

Video also allows a coach to see if players mimic the behaviors of their coach. In working with one coach, his number one complaint about his team was how petulant they were on the soccer field, seemingly whining about every call and constantly blaming others. It took about five minutes of video analysis focused on the coach, and not the players, to see his players were simply doing what he was modeling for them.

A good start to any video work designed to improve self-awareness is to start with the following questions:

- Am I modeling the behavior that I expect?
- Would I be accepting of similar behavior from other people in my program?
- How does a change in my mood or communication style impact my team's performance? Does it do so in the direction I am hoping it moves?
- Does my behavior impact other adults within the program and their behavior?
- Could someone tell the score of the game or the quality of the practice by my behavior? Is that a good or a bad thing?

Chapter 13

Team and Staff Awareness

"A common mistake among those who work in sports is spending a disproportionate amount of time on 'x's and o's' as compared to time spent learning about people." –Mike Krzyzewski

Over the last decade, two rival football programs in northeast Ohio have both inverted their trajectory, leading to a new top dog and dominant program in the region. Northeast Ohio is a football hotbed, producing all-time great athletes and teams, and a place where football is woven into the true fabric of the community.

Northeast High was a perennial powerhouse. Coach Williams and his team seemed to never rebuild. For multiple decades, it seemed they just reloaded and continued to dominate. Other programs in the same conference would have success in pockets, usually borne out of the talent of a superstar or two, but nothing compared to Northeast.

Northeast's chief rival was Taylorville. While Taylorville did not have the history that Northeast did, the rivalry was bitter. This was fueled by the fact that the one time Taylorville won a state title, so did Northeast (in a larger division), but Taylorville had won the regular season between the two, gaining bragging rights. Though Northeast went on to win five more championships in the next fifteen years, and Taylorville to win none, the intensity of the rivalry never waned.

In 2015, Coach Williams won his sixth title and was named to the Ohio Coaches Hall of Fame shortly thereafter. While people were

Chapter 13

impressed with the state title and excited for Coach Williams, the buzz around the program was not about the victorious senior class or about the coach; the buzz was instead focused on the incoming class of freshmen.

This group of kids making their way into the program seemed destined for greatness. Whispers started about this class of tremendous athletes when they were in eighth grade. They had run through the competition for four years in their Junior Tackle league, and everyone was talking about them being the best class to ever come through the school. The future was bright for Northeast.

Conversely, Taylorville did not even qualify for the playoffs in 2015. They had recently hired a hometown kid with no varsity coaching or college playing experience. People were incredibly skeptical of Coach Jackson's hire, and the energy around the program was negative. The two programs could not be in different places.

Through the first two years of high school, the esteemed class from Northeast continued to dominate, losing only a close game to a school with an enrollment nearly three times their size. Meanwhile, Taylorville was making incremental gains but was still very much noted as the little brother to Northeast's big brother. Coach Jackson became known as an old-school coach, not dissimilar to Coach Williams. The town had warmed to him, but people were still skeptical about whether he could get them over the hump.

Northeast's group of freshmen turned into sophomores and became known throughout the small manufacturing community as "The Class." As their sophomore season progressed, many of the more talented players split play time between the junior varsity and varsity teams. The team cruised to a 9–0 record, and during the playoffs, players from "The Class" saw more and more playing time.

Northeast made a deep run losing a heartbreaker in the semifinals. It was one of the few times when a loss breeds hope, as the town buzzed with the excitement of having this juggernaut for two more years. There was widespread consensus that this was Coach Williams's most talented class, and with his Hall of Fame pedigree, Northeast just may be in for two more titles. That would make eight in nineteen years. A true dynasty.

Meanwhile, Taylorville qualified for the playoffs before facing a prompt exit. The future did not look particularly bright in terms of talent, but the consensus was that Taylorville absolutely made the right hire for head coach with Coach Jackson. That said, after year two, he shuffled his coaching staff, hiring multiple people known to be his friends, giving some pause in the community's support of him and the program.

Then, the fortunes of these two programs abruptly switched.

Northeast's downfall was hard to watch. "The Class" was still absurdly talented, but some other athletes in the area certainly caught up to the now upperclassmen at Northeast. That said, talent was not the problem. However, as anyone who has coached at the high school level knows, coaching, leadership, and teamwork are at a premium at the varsity level if you want to be successful. This, most people thought, would remain the distinct advantage of Northeast, given their Hall of Fame coach.

Coach Williams often joked that he coached the way he was coached. He was a hard, no-nonsense type of coach. He was mentored under the "old-school" practices of discipline and hard work and treated each player the same way he was treated. He wasn't one to hold back; and benchwarmer or star, no one was above a good kick in the butt at practice or on the sidelines.

In fact, his approach had earned him more than one "talking to" from the administration in the past. He would adjust but never change. His players loved him. When he was inducted into the Hall of Fame, over two hundred past players came to celebrate him that evening. He was adored.

Coach Williams became so widely known that he often had the opportunity to lead sessions at conferences and workshops on coaching. One thing he would always say is that he could tell how the season would go based on the music in the weight room over the summer. He noted that if the senior leaders took firm control of the stereo and their choices were not challenged, the team would have a great year.

This quip was indicative that Coach Williams expected the players to lead. The leaders of his teams were expected to set the tone and example for the other players. This formula had served him well for nearly twenty years.

Chapter 13

Adhering to this formula, but having no strategy to cultivate it, was the Achilles' heel for "The Class."

Week one of their junior year sent shock waves through Northeast Ohio and changed everything for both Taylorville and Northeast. Northeast was a powerhouse and could find nobody of similar size in the state to play them. As a result, they ended up playing a team from two divisions larger than them who were state semifinalists the year before. Taylorville faced a similar opponent but did so because Coach Jackson sought out bigger opponents to prepare them for the gauntlet of conference play.

Immediately, something was not right. Admittedly, Northeast was overmatched, but Coach Williams's teams have been overmatched before and had never looked like this. Playing against kids that were much bigger, faster, and stronger tested the character of the team. It was clear by halftime that this team lacked character and leadership.

As soon as "The Class" faced difficulty and were trailing in the game, they melted. The same kids who had experienced so much success together for all those years turned on each other. Bickering between teammates and poor body language quickly turned into even worse play.

Coach Williams was beside himself on the sidelines. No matter how much he yelled, no one stepped up and took charge on the field. In fact, the angrier he got, the more bickering and fighting happened on the field. Northeast was crushed—both on the field and in the locker room after week one.

Coach Jackson, another old-school, hard-nosed coach, was seen getting on the bus in a seventies-style leisure suit as Taylorville decided to do a bit of "dress up" on their way to central Ohio to play their own challenging game. And, wow, did they ever play! Taylorville came out using an offense they had not used in over twenty years.

Taylorville flew around the field all night long. Kids were smiling. Coach Jackson was a high-five machine. Taylorville upset a state-ranked opponent in a larger class—the Taylorville football program rebuild was officially on track. After the game, Coach Jackson was interviewed on the local news—in his leisure suit. He remarked that he had a high-strung group of athletes as a collective, giving that as the reason he wanted everyone to dress up on the bus. He admitted to seeing it work for Joe

Maddon and the Cubs, so he thought it was worth a try to lighten the kids up on the long bus ride. Clearly, it worked.

For the next two years, this same scenario played out over and over again for both teams. Coach Williams stayed the course and did not adjust based on his players and their lack of natural leadership. Coach Jackson continued to change to meet the needs of his players and to amplify the skills of the assistant coaches he had hired and knew deeply.

At the end of "The Class's" varsity careers, they never even made the playoffs. This was supposed to be the group that was destined to be the greatest in Coach Williams's tenure at Northeast. Taylorville had two semifinal appearances. Little brother became big brother. One coach adjusted to the strengths and needs of his team. One coach expected the team to adjust to his philosophy and style. The results speak for themselves.

CRACKING THE COACHING CODE

To be a great coach, there is a laundry list of traits and skills that one must possess. There are tactical skills, organizational skills, and time management skills that every great coach must have. Beyond these skills, however, awareness is paramount.

As discussed in the last chapter, self-awareness is the first ingredient of success. If we do not know ourselves and value and nurture that intrapersonal relationship, every other relationship we are a part of will be negatively impacted. To move from an average coach to a good coach, self-awareness and self-mastery are necessary.

Additionally, however, there is one skill that seems to separate the good from the great. A characteristic seen with all great coaches is their deep understanding of who their players and staff are and their willingness to adjust their methods in order to lead them accordingly.

Said directly, an average coach expects their players to adjust to them. A great coach adjusts their systems to best meet the needs of their players. Most coaches intuitively know this but largely think of it schematically. Our challenge to you is to think about this in terms of leadership, as much as you think about it in terms of x's and o's.

Chapter 13

A great example of this is Bill Belichick, coach of the New England Patriots. Coach Belichick is arguably the greatest football coach of all time, having won eight Super Bowls in his time as a head coach and defensive coordinator.

From the surface, it's easy to see why he has had so much success. He checks all the boxes. He has all the skills and knowledge, is tactically savvy, has a deep self-awareness, and is impervious to the outside noise that would only serve to distract him from his primary purpose.

A hallmark of Coach Belichick's teams is that there are very few stars surrounded by athletes that come with much less fanfare or have been cast aside by other teams for behavioral issues or distractions they cause the team. Coach Belichick does not seek out the coveted high-priced coaching sensations. He rarely hires externally, instead preferring to promote from within.

He has mastered the ability to see who someone is and who they can become. He then coaches them in the way they need to be coached.

With both his athletes and his coaches, he takes ownership of his responsibility to put people in positions to be successful. In order to do so, he must know their strengths and weaknesses, and also make sure they do. Moreover, he must have an acute knowledge of how the collection of strengths and weaknesses on the team and coaching staff fit together. His unmatched ability to recognize this allows him to change to meet the needs of the team based on his assessment of where gaps fit.

People often talk about the "Patriot Way" or Coach Belichick's mantra of, "Do your job." This is just shorthand for explaining that he never asks anyone, player or coach, to be or do anything that is outside of who they truly are. The beauty of this, however, is that for this to work he must deeply and sincerely know who they truly are.

From the outside, his teams are boring. Everyone follows the system and puts the team first. As a result, emotions are subdued, and as a public consuming content, it becomes hard to get to know the players. It appears to be all business and no fun.

But, if you read about or listen to interviews about him, he has a great connection to his players and coaches. No story better amplifies this than that of Randy Moss. Randy Moss was an enigmatic and controversial player dating back to his high school days. Still, the Patriots went out of their way to acquire the talented wide receiver.

While a member of the Patriots, Moss had such a relationship with Coach Belichick that he once invited him to a Halloween party at a roller rink. There is a great video from this party of Coach Belichick, dressed like a pirate, roller skating, demonstrating the connection and understanding that he needed to have to adapt to meet his players where they were at. At that particular moment, they needed to see him as a human being.

This ability to see people for who they are and adapt to meet their needs is why he is able to put his team and players in a position to be successful year after year. Additionally, later in Moss's tenure, he became a distraction, and Belichick promptly traded one of the best players in the league. This move appeared to indicate that he believed in addition by subtraction, and he could only make such a move if he understood the psyche of his collective team.

Now, the knock on Coach Belichick is that none of his coaches have been able to duplicate his success when they went on to coach their own teams. In fact, most of them have crashed and burned wherever they have ended up, with many returning to the Patriots to resurrect their careers.

While this seems like a downside, there is a very simple explanation for why this happens. Each one of them tries to duplicate his system and tactics. This leaves them cold, calculated, and all business. Seemingly, his protégés have failed to learn the real lesson. Knowing your players and coaches, who they are and what they can do, comes first. Then, make sure *they* know who they are and what they can do. Then, be adaptable in order to push them to their limits.

The failure to adapt and respond to the needs of his players and coaches is what led to diminished outcomes for Coach Williams. His system ran perfectly when he had kids on the team that were natural leaders. He could rely on them to show the others how to work hard, play hard, and pick each other up.

When "The Class" came through, he had a team full of individuals that were so accustomed to their talent being superior to their opponents that they never learned how to lead, depend on each other, or work as a collective. Once they ran into any adversity, they started to play the blame game instead of taking accountability. Instead of adjusting to the personalities and behaviors of his team, Coach Williams stayed the course, as he had throughout his career.

If Coach Williams took the time to understand the needs of his individual players, coaches, and the collective team, he would have recognized that there were no natural leaders. He then could have coached them differently, and, ultimately, put them in positions to be successful.

The juxtaposition of Coach Williams and Coach Jackson is clear. Both in terms of tactics and demeanor, Coach Jackson was the one who constantly adjusted. He did not expect the players to meet him where he was; he met them where they were. Success followed the coach and the team that was willing to adapt.

In summation, not everyone can be treated the same way. In fact, no two people can be treated the same way, and certainly no two teams.

Some kids you have to yell at to get the most out of. Some kids will be crippled if you do so.

Some kids just need to be told what to do and will never question a coach's authority. Some kids need to understand the "why."

Some kids love to do the dirty work, like block or play defense. Some kids are motivated by headlines and stat sheets.

Some kids want the ball when the game is on the line and the clock is winding down. Some kids don't want any part of that.

Some kids want to lead. Some kids are fearful of the responsibility.

Some kids are vocal and communicative. Some kids would rather never speak and lead by example.

The same types of things can be said about assistant coaches. Some are quiet and creative, while others are aggressive and full of energy to fire up the team. Still, others are empathic and can create great connections with certain players, and others are socially awkward tactical geniuses.

Your job as a coach is to identify who they are and put them in a position where they can be successful. You'll see all different kinds of athletes, coaches, and leaders. If you treat each one of them the same, you'll alienate more members of your team than you will actually reach. You are the one that must be aware of others and adjust, not them.

The Five Activities to Increase Your Team's and Staff's Awareness

We know what most of you are thinking at this point, "How am I going to do all this, and get ready for the game on Saturday?"

Thinking about digging deep and really getting to know all of your players and coaches can seem daunting. It can also seem like a waste of time. After all, you can't help but wonder how knowing the Enneagram type of your midfielder is going to make him execute your set piece any better in the last ninety seconds of a tie game.

This, however, is exactly the purpose of knowing your personnel.

If that midfielder is a Type 5, then they are probably calm no matter what the circumstances are and can be trusted to make the right decision without much intervention or coaching. If your midfielder is a Type 2, they can likely be trusted to defer on a direct kick and make a pass that helps their teammate get open. If your star midfielder is a Type 6, you may elect someone else to take the corner kick because they can be trusted to do the dirty work and set the screen that helps your forward get the open shot. And the midfielder, who is a Type 8, and wants the ball with the game on the line, won't hesitate when the time comes.

I don't care how the play is drawn up, its success will be exponentially higher with that level of insight in your players.

Again, it all comes down to trust and knowing who your players and staff are. Here are five tools for you to use to increase not only your awareness of your players and staff but their awareness of themselves as well.

1. Teach them the Enneagram.

    Coaches for the most part have almost unlimited access to classes, workshops, and retreats to gain the skills to be a coach. A quick internet search will lead to countless examples of the best type of offense run against a zone defense, the best training regime for a 400m runner, or the perfect zone blitz. You can even find thousands of books, seminars, and podcasts dedicated to leadership. But what has been missing is a system, or training, on figuring out who your players are.

Chapter 13

How do you determine if they are natural leaders or if they prefer to be part of the crowd? Which players can you tell to run through the wall, and which ones do you need to fire up to do the same? How do you know if that assistant is going to freeze up when the game is on the line and call the wrong play, costing you the game, or if they are so heated on the sideline they get a technical, changing the momentum?

This is the differentiator between coaches that are vying for championships every year, and the ones that finish in the bottom half of the conference year after year. They know their players.

The problem is that too frequently this is left to chance or innate talent or will. The Enneagram provides a systematic approach to cracking this code and amplifying our coaching talent. It is the perfect system to not only identify your own weaker areas and default behaviors but also can help identify others' as well.

If you don't think this information will be valuable, ask yourself these three questions:

- How would your team perform if everyone (from the head coach down to the statistician) knew their specific role on the team and how their personality profile can help them achieve success?
- How would each player's performance change if they had an understanding of how they responded during times of adversity or great success or flow?
- What would your team look like if each player and coach knew exactly what the person standing next to them would do with the game on the line?

The Enneagram will not only allow you to have a better awareness of your team and your staff, but it will also build trust among them. Trust is built on several factors, including reliability. Reliability refers to whether or not we can predict how others will react when things become difficult. There is no greater tool to build this understanding than the Enneagram.

Team and Staff Awareness

While we believe there is no greater way for you to learn something than to teach it, there is value in having an outside expert or organization work through this process with your team. If you choose to go it alone, we believe that, since you have read the book and done some of the exercises from the previous chapters, you will be ready.

Start with a free RHETI exam found online and begin to work through the process of teaching your team what you have learned through this book. Remember, Enneagram is a process of self-discovery first. Internal victory must exist before external victory. That said, this tool will create a point of leverage that will allow you to better understand your players and coaches, and unlock their peak performance potential.

1. Engage in a "pre-season" focused team-building.

Organize an event shortly before the season begins to gain a deeper understanding of what type of players you have. The objective for the day is simple. Create programming that will push your team to their limits mentally and physically. To do this, fill the day with challenges, both physical and mental.

> Ideally, you can have other coaches (outside of your program or from an outside entity) set this up and run the day. This allows you to simply observe. Additionally, this also allows you to have your assistants participate in the programming without prior knowledge of what is taking place or the insights you hope to gain.
>
> Use games like tug of war, the helium stick, blanket volleyball, team skis, or any type of relay race. The goal is to create activities that really bring out different autopilot behaviors. After a while, you'll begin to notice the same people stepping forward to organize or lead the group, and you'll see a similar group step back and just go with the flow. You'll notice those incentivized by rewards and those focused on helping others. Every piece of behavioral insight you gain helps you to better support your people and adjust your leadership tactics accordingly.

2. Create four-tier practice plans with corresponding observations.

CHAPTER 13

You can set up either full practices or sessions in practice that are as follows:

- Coach led
- Captain led
- Collaboratively led
- Free play

These practices are twofold in intent. While most practices focus on skill development and preparation for future contests these *occasional* designated practices also allow for insight into your players. To be specific, the call to action here is to design a practice or to observe a practice with a focus solely on behavioral interactions, and not on skill assessment and development.

Conducting this type of observation in four different settings allows for unique takeaways. For instance, there is a lot to be learned when someone follows every rule, regardless of who is running a practice. There is a lot to learn when someone who is not a captain attempts to take over a captain's practice. The examples are endless, but a coach giving themselves permission to observe behavior and creating different conditions in which to inspect that behavior will lead to incredible insights into the personalities and behaviors of all members of the team.

3. Review film.

Film never lies. If you want to get the best out of your practices, they should be filmed and reviewed just like your games. Use your film session review to not only correct mistakes made in games and practices but as collaborative learning sessions on behavior. Specifically look for body language, aggression, hesitation, or outright freezing.

As an aside, in the past twenty years, practices for many sports and in many regions have dramatically decreased in terms of duration. There is science to support that having a three-hour practice day after day may be counterproductive to peak performance for young athletes. Shortened physical practices do, however, tend to leave ample time for video review if you are serious about bringing forth the best possible performance of your coaches and athletes.

4. Bring in outside entities to observe both practice and games.

   This technique is the cousin to strategy three. In our work with coaches, the concept of giving up practice time focused on skill development to watch behavior is often met with (at best) skepticism. While we believe in that strategy, an alternative is to use outside resources to invert the roles.

   To explain, have someone from outside the program (athletic director, mentor, another coach, a parent, community member, etc.) observe the practice and look for behavioral tendencies while you continue to focus on skill development and game preparation.

   The outside entity should be looking for the following:

- Attitude
- How does everyone respond to a bad call? (As a coach you can intentionally create this situation.)
- How does someone respond to in-game coaching? Does their response change based on the intensity or style of coaching?
- What is the team's demeanor when losing? Does any individual stick out as an outlier, either positively or negatively?
- How do your assistant coaches act when mistakes are made?
- Does body language or intangibles (communication) change when losing? Winning?
- What is the communication like? Coach to player? Teammate to teammate? Player to coach?
- What kind of language is used to communicate? Positive and encouraging? Negative and demeaning? Coach to coach? Coach to player? Teammate to teammate?

CHAPTER 14

Situational Awareness

"You can't always control circumstances. However, you can always control your attitude, approach, and response. Your options are to complain or to look ahead and figure out how to make the situation better." –Tony Dungy

Situational awareness is something that we all have. Technically, situational awareness refers to our ability to rationalize and make meaning of the environmental elements and events happening around us and to understand how the combination of everything going on may impact the future.

Effective leaders must be situationally aware. Context matters. Situational awareness, as it pertains to leadership, is the ability to take in all of that information and then have the cognition to choose your behaviors to best create the outcome you so desire. To take this from the theoretical to the practical, three researchers (Jordan, Wade, and Teracino) featured in the *Harvard Business Review* identified seven real-time tensions all leaders must consider when attempting to improve their situational awareness. The seven tensions are as follows:

- To be the expert or to be the learner
- To be the constant or to be the adapter
- To be the tactician or to be the visionary
- To be the teller or to be the listener
- To be the power-holder or to be the power-sharer

- To be the intuitionist or to be the analyst
- To be the perfectionist or to be the accelerator

Effective leaders must not only be able to make an accurate read of their environment but they must also identify the internal tension that will undoubtedly arise as they determine their next course of action. As you should have surmised by now, based on your Enneagram type, your default behavior is going to lead you toward behaving in certain ways if you are left on autopilot and not situationally aware.

For instance, an Enneagram Type 8, when simply functioning on autopilot, will not have the situational awareness to make the decision to be the power-sharer, instead of the power-holder. As emotional intelligence and situational awareness grow, behavior will change to better align with your overall objectives, instead of the default results you have been used to getting for years.

The point is, increasing your situational awareness will change your outcomes. You have to be aware of who you are and who each individual on your team and on your staff is, and then use that information to plot out your next chess move, in order to get the most out of your team.

Miracle

In the 2004 Disney depiction of the 1984 USA hockey victory over the Russian national team entitled *Miracle*, the brilliance and strategy used by Coach Herb Brooks becomes one of the main storylines of the movie. No scene in the movie better encapsulates his situational awareness and ability to not act on autopilot than the intermission scene while the U.S. hockey team is playing Sweden in the Olympics.

Brooks has a calm and measured conversation with his assistant coaches before and immediately after his interaction with the team. When he approaches the team he is visibly angry and flips a table. He proceeds to challenge one of the players, who was ruled out of the game with a bad bone bruise on his leg, making the comment that the injury is a "long way from the heart." As an aside, this has become common phraseology around our houses.

After Coach Brooks has seemingly lost his temper and is acting out of pure emotion and without control, the rant in front of the players ends. Coach Brooks then goes into the next room and calmly asks his assistant coach, with a sly grin, "Do you think that will get them going?"

While we do not subscribe to the fact that you need to flip tables or challenge the toughness of your team to be a great coach, we do believe that you need to adjust your behavior to the context of the situation in order to get the results you desire. Brooks did this masterfully by feigning anger. He perceived a lack of energy and commitment from his team and felt that the way to up the intensity of his players was, in this particularly unique situation, to portray anger.

In this scene, Brooks does the near impossible. He remains in complete control by ostensibly losing control. He was playing chess as a leader, not checkers. This is what situational awareness is all about.

Four Prerequisites to Stay Situationally Aware

In the previous chapters of this book, we have provided strategies on how to become more aware of yourself and your team. In an attempt to provide some tangible takeaways for situational awareness, the focus of this chapter will be on creating reminders and a protocol necessary to remain situationally aware.

1. SLAM: Stop, Look, Assess, Manage

    This means being cognizant of all that is going on around you and being willing to manage or lead differently to create the outcomes you desire. A football coach was explaining at a clinic a few weeks ago that he had run the same play (Fullback Belly) on 4th and 1 all year with over a 90 percent success rate. He noted he was leveraging his all-state interior linemen and his all-area fullback with supreme confidence all year.

    He admitted, however, that with three minutes to go in the conference title game, he instead ran a play-action pass from his own twenty-eight. When a different coach asked if this decision was to throw off the tendency he used all year and to confuse the other coach, he shook his head no and simply said that his boys were gassed and the other team was not wearing down. He did not believe his squad was going to be able to move the ball the seventy additional yards necessary to score without a big play of some sort.

Given that assessment, he took a chance and brought home a conference championship after the team recorded their longest completion of the year. Coach took a minute (STOP) and monitored his team (LOOK), making the determination that they were exhausted (ASSESS), so he deviated from his autopilot behavior (FB Belly). He was situationally aware.

2. Attention directs awareness

A coach that was working so hard to build discipline and competitive toughness with his team was on the precipice of his biggest win to date. This could have been a win that turned the fortunes of the season, and perhaps, the program completely around. As his star point guard was dribbling the ball in a tie game with eight seconds left, the right side of the court opened up, and the star player began to attack. Simultaneously, the coach called for a timeout.

As the coach grabbed the dry-erase board to draw up the game-winning play, the star player loudly cussed out the coach on his way to the bench. The outburst was loud enough for people several rows up in the crowd to hear the rant word for word. The coach seemed impervious and drew up a play that led to the game-winning shot.

The immediate exaltation was immediately sullied. The conversation between the players and parents after the game had to do with the player's behavior and the coach's lack of holding his player accountable, instead of the game-winning shot.

In this situation, the coach would have advised any other coach to not put that player back into the game to take the last shot. He was so overwhelmed by the moment and all of his attention was on the final play that he did not hold firm to the core tenets of the program, which he was fighting to establish. Attention directs awareness. When we lose ourselves in the moment, we do just that. We lose ourselves and our self-awareness.

3. Trust your gut, but verify

    Situational awareness takes a team. Sincerely, in many instances of leadership, whether it be school leadership, corporate leadership, or political leadership, events happen at a considerably slower pace than they do in the athletic arena. As a school leader, I may have weeks to consider, analyze, think through, and collaborate on a key decision. As a coach, that may all happen in five seconds. Thus, the need for support and guidance.

    This is why in the situation described above, an assistant coach should have pulled the coach aside and helped him see the entire situation before he made any key decisions. When things are happening at an incredible speed all around you, whatever level of maturity your situational awareness may be at, you will need a team of people all pulling in the same direction, in order to make the best possible decisions.

4. Fight the urge to project

    For more people, their immediate perception of an event is simply projection. Meaning, most people assign meaning to an event based on how they would respond to it. To be situationally aware, a leader or coach must be aware of the context, themselves, and those they have the privilege of coaching. Thus, in order to be situationally aware, we must first understand that we cannot fall into the trap of projecting our default reactions onto every situation.

    As a coach or a leader, once we project our default responses, and worse, expect those responses to be the responses of others, we have lost our ability to lead in dynamic situations. The world does not go as scripted. No game or competition can go precisely as planned. Even practices have hiccups and complications. In order to be a great coach, you must fight against yourself to ensure your reactions and projections do not cloud your ability to be a situationally aware leader.

Chapter 14

The Goal

In order to crack the coaching code, you must increase your overall awareness. The entire thesis of this book is that increasing your ability to understand yourself and who you are on autopilot will increase your effectiveness. This effectiveness will be magnified to absurd amplitude if you are able to also learn how to better understand your players. We offer the Enneagram tool as a wonderful resource to use in this personal and collective journey. The purpose of this chapter, however, is simple. You can know Enneagram backward and forward, but until you use it to increase your self-awareness, your team awareness, and your situational awareness, it will remain an interesting tool.

When you start to use the Enneagram to help yourself move from autopilot, you can help your players reach peak performance by understanding how to better communicate with them and connect at a different level. Once accomplished, incredible change will occur. This combination will directly lead to an increase in situational awareness that will make you a better leader and coach in both controlled situations and in real-life, unpredictable situations. This is how we crack the coaching code.

Chapter 15

Call to Action

Throughout this book, we have focused on the difficult process of increasing your self-awareness and provided the tools necessary to better relate to your players and tailor your approach to crack the coaching code and move them closer to peak performance. As we were reviewing the manuscript, we thought we would be remiss if we did not acknowledge other key components that impact coaches at the high school and college levels.

This section of the book is very short and is in no way a complete exploration of these other key components of the job, but we wanted to acknowledge these other components to show how better knowing yourself and having a deep knowledge of Enneagram can help you in these other core components of the job, as well.

All successful coaches also master and have successful relationships with parents, successful relationships with and administration, successfully recruit athletes, and have definitive skills when it comes to game planning and "x's and o's." Our hope is that throughout this book we have provided you with enough information that you have gotten to know yourselves better.

To give one example, using the four areas above, we will explore game planning to clearly make our point. If you truly have grown in your self-awareness, it will be apparent to you how your personality impacts each area—inclusive of the one that is the least relationship-based: game planning.

One of our favorite sayings is "I bring all of me wherever I go." This simple quote underscores the importance of self-awareness. As you develop game plans, are you hyperaggressive, concerned with looking "pretty," or always focused on solving the problems your opponent will create? After reading this book, our hope is that you start to see that you may be predisposed to one of these styles. The beauty of what we hope you have learned is that you do not have to be. *Your personality does not have to dictate your behavior.*

Your Calling

We have never met a coach that simply wants to be average. We have never met a coach that does not want to better connect with their players. We have never met a *successful* coach that loved the game more than they loved the players that called them Coach.

In our experience, both inside and outside of athletics, the thing that separates incredibly successful leaders from everyone else is the ability to understand and adapt to the humans we have the privilege of leading. The title of this book was chosen for a reason; we believe that Enneagram gives us an advantage that few people choose to use or even know about. We believe that if you choose to use Enneagram, you can crack the code and become the best possible Coach you can be.

The methodology is simple. In every situation, we ask that you take a moment to assess using the R^3 process. When you review, reset, and then resolve, you provide yourself with the opportunity to best serve your athletes and your own interests as a coach. By doing so, you give yourself an opportunity to increase your self-awareness, team awareness, and situational awareness. If you do so, you can be totally present in the moment and best serve your athletes.

Lastly, while the focus of this book is on getting to know your athletes so that you can differentiate your tactics to induce peak performance, none of that will be possible without taking the time to better know yourself. Our hope is that this book helps you to take a deep look in the mirror to find your own blind spots and how you operate when on autopilot. If you have internal victory first, you will undoubtedly become a better leader for those you serve, and you will have a chance for external victory and better serving your players.

So, dig deep into Enneagram, and dig deep into getting to better know yourself and your players. If you do so, you will crack the coaching code. You will find as your work toward increasing your self-awareness deepens that your personality is largely a collection of internal defenses and reactions, deeply ingrained beliefs, and habits of yourself and the world. This understanding will allow you to realize that you are not your personality and that you can choose to alter your behaviors and tendencies to help yourself, and others, move toward peak performance.

The Next Step

Thank you for taking the time to read our book, *Cracking the Coaching Code*. We hope that it has been informative and has provided you with valuable insights into how to become a better coach and help your athletes reach their full potential.

As you may have noticed, our book only scratches the surface of what self-awareness and the Enneagram can offer in the world of sports coaching. If you're interested in learning more about these topics and how they can help you become an even better coach, we encourage you to visit our website at www.crackingthecoachingcode.com.

There, you will find a wealth of information and resources on the Enneagram, self-awareness, and athletic coaching. We have developed online courses, workshops, and coaching sessions that will help you dive deeper into these subjects and put what you've learned into practice.

We understand that coaching is a challenging and demanding profession. That's why we believe that investing in your own personal development is essential to helping your athletes succeed. By becoming more self-aware and understanding the personalities and motivations of your athletes, you'll be better equipped to build stronger relationships, communicate more effectively, and create a more positive and productive team culture.

So, if you are looking to have a greater impact both on and off the field, we urge you to take action now and visit our website. Together, we can create a world of self-aware and empathetic coaches who bring out the best in their athletes.

About the Authors

Dr. PJ Caposey is the Illinois superintendent of the year and a best-selling author, having written nine books for various publishers. His work and commentary have been featured on sites such as TED, *The Washington Post*, NPR, CBS *This Morning*, ASCD, *Edutopia*, *The Huffington Post (HuffPost)*, and have been featured in think pieces alongside General Petraeus and General McChrystal. PJ is a sought-after presenter and consultant who recently keynoted several national conferences with expertise in time management, the tyranny of the status quo, school culture, continuous improvement, and teacher evaluation.

Dr. Bryan Wills is a chiropractor, entrepreneur, executive coach, and dynamic speaker. Bryan opened his first chiropractic office right after he graduated from Palmer College of Chiropractic in a rural community in northern Illinois. He has gone on to open up two more highly successful practices in Rockford, Illinois, built with the same small-town values of Family, Integrity, and Authenticity, as the original.

From the experience Bryan gained in starting multiple businesses from scratch, he decided to help others by becoming an executive coach in 2015. Since then, Bryan has been able to help hundreds of people chase after their dreams of becoming entrepreneurs and business owners.

Teaching and speaking have been passions of Bryan's since the beginning. He has been fortunate enough to speak to chiropractors, business owners, and entrepreneurs throughout the country. Entertaining and engaging, Bryan focuses most of his presentations on personal growth, success principles, and business systems and philosophy.

www.ingramcontent.com/pod-product-compliance
Lightning Source LLC
Chambersburg PA
CBHW032024230426
43671CB00005B/196